Visual Studio 2012 Cookbook

50 simple but incredibly effective recipes to immediately get you working with the exciting features of Visual Studio 2012

Richard Banks

PUBLISHING

BIRMINGHAM - MUMBAI

Visual Studio 2012 Cookbook

First published: September 2012

Production Reference: 1290812

Published by Packt Publishing Ltd.
Livery Place
35 Livery Street
Birmingham B3 2PB, UK.

ISBN 978-1-84968-652-5

www.packtpub.com

Cover Image by David Gimenez (bilbaorocker@yahoo.co.uk)

Credits

Author

Richard Banks

Reviewers

Dave McKinstry

Quinten Miller

Anand Narayanaswamy

Justin "JT" Taylor

Acquisition Editor

Stephanie Moss

Lead Technical Editor

Kedar Bhat

Technical Editor

Joyslita D'Souza

Project Coordinator

Joel Goveya

Proofreader

Kevin McGowan

Indexer

Monica Ajmera Mehta

Production Coordinator

Melwyn D'sa

Cover Work

Melwyn D'sa

Foreword

When we sat down to map out the next version of our premier software development tool, Microsoft Visual Studio 2012, we had a few key scenarios in mind.

One of those scenarios was Developers are Raving Fans. We clearly heard the feedback about the speed of Visual Studio, about the discoverability of features, its ability to support ever changing and improving engineering practices, and various other sources of frustration. With Microsoft Visual Studio 2012 we wanted to not only address that feedback but to then go on and exceed people's expectations as to what Visual Studio can do for them. We wanted to surprise and delight them with the features on offer and to give them both the reason and opportunity to fall back in love with the software they use every day.

We also wanted developers to regard Visual Studio as a key enabler in developing fantastic experiences for Windows 8 and not as a tax on their development efforts. We wanted them to enjoy the process of developing world changing software and to make it eminently approachable; not just for those familiar with Visual Studio but also for those who are new to Windows development.

We believe we have met these goals, and then some.

Richard's book is a perfect complement to Visual Studio 2012 for both the experienced and new Visual Studio developer alike. It is highly approachable and educational and is a book that you can pick up and use immediately in your daily development efforts. The cookbook style recipe format helps you quickly get to grips with how Microsoft Visual Studio 2012 can be used for building fantastic software and answers the key question you have, which is "What's new in Microsoft Visual Studio 2012?".

Brian Harry
Technical Fellow, Microsoft Corporation

About the Author

Richard Banks has developed software for the last 20 years for a wide range of industries and development platforms and over the years has filled many roles including Developer, Team Lead, Project Manager, and CIO/CTO. He is a Professional Scrum Trainer, runs the Sydney Alt.Net user group and the Talking Shop Down Under podcast, owns and contributes to a few open source projects, and has spoken at Microsoft Tech.Ed and a number of other events and user groups around Australia. For some strange reason he gets a real kick out of helping development teams to improve and produce great software. If you want to get in touch, his tweet handle is `@rbanks54`. He blogs at `http://www.richard-banks.org/`. He currently works as a Principal Consultant for Readify and is a Microsoft Visual Studio ALM MVP.

It might have my name on the front cover but a book is never the work of just one person.

I would firstly like to thank my fantastic wife, Anne, and my two wonderful children, Hannah and Leisel, for giving me the time and space to work on this book. Their support throughout the process has been invaluable and without that I would have never undertaken this book in the first place.

I'd also like to thank the staff of Packt Publishing for the opportunity and help in bringing this together, and my tech reviewers who gave up their spare time reading my scribble and checking that what I wrote actually made sense, instead of being just a delirium fuelled pile of nonsense.

Thank you all!

About the Reviewers

Dave McKinstry has over 20 years professional experience in computer systems, including programming and system administration on VAX minicomputers through development and architecture in Microsoft technologies. For the past dozen years, he has been helping clients adopt modern technologies and best practices for application development.

He is currently the ALM practice manager for Microsoft's 2011 ALM Partner of the year, Imaginet Resources. Before merging with Imaginet, he was a founding partner with Notion Solutions.

He was a Technical Reviewer on *Architecting Web Services* (ISBN 1-893115-58-5).

> Thank you to my wife, Liana and my son for their patience with this and all of my other "side-projects".

Anand Narayanaswamy is an ASPInsider who works as a freelance technical writer based in Trivandrum, India. He has worked as a Technical Editor/Reviewer for various publishers such as Sams, Addison-Wesley, Mc Graw Hill, Packt Publishing, and ASPAlliance.com. He has expertise in the installation, management, and usage of popular ASP.NET and PHP based blogs/Content Management Systems (CMS). He is the author of *Community Server Quickly* (www.packtpub.com/community-server/book) published by Packt Publishing, and can be reached at visualanand@gmail.com. His tweet handle is @anandenclave.

> First, I would like to thank the Almighty for giving me the strength and energy to work every day. I would specially like to thank my father, mother, and brother for providing valuable help, support, and encouragement. I would also like to thank Joel Goveya, Project Coordinator at Packt Publishing, for his assistance, cooperation, and understanding throughout the review process of this book.

Justin "JT" Taylor has been developing software for fun and profit for the last 12 years. He has worked on a variety of technologies throughout his career, but most recently has focused his craft on utilizing Microsoft XAML based technologies, WPF, Silverlight, and WinRT. Working with Readify, he provides opinions (of which he has many) and expertise to clients to help them get the most out of their software development efforts. He prefers to remain somewhat nomadic in nature, changing his place of residence as fast as the landscape of the industry he loves so much. If he weren't working in the software industry, he would most like to be caped and cowled, fighting crime on the mean streets of Gotham City.

www.PacktPub.com

Support files, eBooks, discount offers, and more

You might want to visit www.PacktPub.com for support files and downloads related to your book.

Did you know that Packt offers eBook versions of every book published, with PDF and ePub files available? You can upgrade to the eBook version at www.PacktPub.com and as a print book customer, you are entitled to a discount on the eBook copy. Get in touch with us at service@packtpub.com for more details.

At www.PacktPub.com, you can also read a collection of free technical articles, sign up for a range of free newsletters and receive exclusive discounts and offers on Packt books and eBooks.

http://PacktLib.PacktPub.com

Do you need instant solutions to your IT questions? PacktLib is Packt's online digital book library. Here, you can access, read and search across Packt's entire library of books.

Why Subscribe?

- ▶ Fully searchable across every book published by Packt
- ▶ Copy and paste, print and bookmark content
- ▶ On demand and accessible via web browser

Free Access for Packt account holders

If you have an account with Packt at www.PacktPub.com, you can use this to access PacktLib today and view nine entirely free books. Simply use your login credentials for immediate access.

Table of Contents

Preface   **1**

Chapter 1: Discovering Visual Studio 2012   **5**

Introduction   5
Creating a new project   5
Upgrading an existing solution   8
Managing editor windows   11
Finding Visual Studio commands   16
Navigating and searching   19
Searching your code   23
Using the graphics tools   25

Chapter 2: Getting Started with Windows Store Applications   **31**

Introduction   31
Creating a Windows Store app   33
Adding a Windows Store item template to your app   40
Using the Windows 8 simulator   44
Defining capabilities and contracts   52
Packaging your Windows Store app   58
Validating your Windows Store app   63

Chapter 3: Web Development: ASP.NET, HTML5, CSS, and JavaScript   **65**

Introduction   65
Creating HTML5 web pages   66
Taking advantage of CSS editor improvements   70
Understanding the JavaScript editor improvements   75
JavaScript and CSS bundling and minification   79
Verifying pages with the Page Inspector   84

Chapter 4: .NET Framework 4.5 Development   91

Introduction   91
Adding the Ribbon to a WPF application   92
Creating a state machine in Visual Studio 2012   97
Creating a Task-based WCF service   103
Managing packages with NuGet   107
Unit testing .NET applications   111
Sharing class libraries across runtimes   117
Detecting duplicate code   119

Chapter 5: Debugging Your .NET Application   125

Introduction   125
Debugging on remote machines and tablets   126
Debugging code in production   133
Debugging parallel code   139
Visualizing concurrency   144

Chapter 6: Asynchrony in .NET   149

Introduction   149
Making your code asynchronous   150
Asynchrony and Windows Runtime   156
Asynchrony and web applications   161
Actors and the TPL Dataflow Library   165

Chapter 7: Unwrapping C++ Development   171

Introduction   171
Using XAML with C++   172
Unit testing C++ applications   175
Analyzing your C++ code   180
Working with DirectX in Visual Studio 2012   182
Creating a shader using DGSL   186
Creating and displaying a 3D model   191
Using the Visual Studio Graphics Debugger   194

Chapter 8: Working with Team Foundation Server 2012   201

Introduction   201
Managing your work   202
Using local workspaces for source control   207
Storyboarding user requirements   214
Performing code reviews   219
Getting feedback from your users   225

Appendix: Visual Studio Pot Pourri   231

Introduction   231

Creating installer packages   231

Submitting apps to the Windows Store   236

Using the new SQL Server Data Tools   239

Creating Visual Studio add-ins and extensions   242

Creating your own snippets   244

Index   249

Preface

Visual Studio 2012 Cookbook is a set of simple-to-follow recipes that you can use to discover and master the features of the latest version of Microsoft's premier development tool.

While you could try and discover features by clicking around in the menus, it's easy to miss the new features and to see how they can help you. Plus Visual Studio 2012 has so much more to offer than just features that can be accessed via menu entries. The recipes in this book will help you quickly get up to speed with what those features are, how they work, and how you might use them to produce fantastic software in less time than you thought possible.

What this book covers

Chapter 1, Discovering Visual Studio 2012, introduces you to the common IDE features that you can take advantage of, regardless of the language you are developing in or the type of software you are building. Discover the new project types, navigation options, search facilities, and more.

Chapter 2, Getting Started with Windows Store Applications, shows you how Visual Studio 2012—the only way you can build the new modern style apps for Windows 8—supports Windows Store app development, how the simulator works, and how to package up an application for submission to the Windows Store.

Chapter 3, Web Development: ASP.NET, HTML5, CSS, and JavaScript, brings you up to speed with the wide ranging improvements in web development that Visual Studio 2012 brings to the table. This includes the CSS and JavaScript editing improvements, the new Page Inspector, and the bundling and minification features in ASP.NET.

Chapter 4, .NET Framework 4.5 Development, shows you how Visual Studio 2012 provides outstanding support for the .NET Framework 4.5 development and touches on some of the new key features in the framework. You will also be shown how Visual Studio 2012 helps you raise the quality of the code you build using the new Test Explorer and code clone detection features.

Chapter 5, Debugging Your .NET Application, steps you through the new and improved debugging capabilities of Visual Studio 2012. These include the new production debugging capability and improved ways of understanding what your parallel and concurrent code is doing.

Chapter 6, Asynchrony in .NET, takes a deeper look into the support Visual Studio 2012 provides for writing asynchronous code in .NET so that you can make better use of multi-core machines to improve your application's responsiveness and performance. You will see how the async and await keywords make development much simpler and how new libraries such as the TPL DataFlow library can open up new ways of solving concurrency problems.

Chapter 7, Unwrapping C++ Development, gives you an insight into Visual Studio 2012's fresh love for C++ developers, the new language features it supports, and the tooling to make developing C++ applications quicker. You will see how you can mix C++ and XAML to build a Windows Store app UI, how to unit test and analyze your code, and how to diagnose how a single pixel was drawn to screen in DirectX apps.

Chapter 8, Working with Team Foundation Server 2012, guides you through both the Team Foundation Server 2012 and Visual Studio 2012 improvements for team-based development, and agile development in particular. This includes source control, code reviews, gaining feedback from your users, and more.

Appendix, Visual Studio Pot Pourri, is all about the wonderful features of Visual Studio 2012 that didn't really fit anywhere else but that are still of great value. This includes features such as the new SQL Server Developer Tools, the creation of application installers, and how to submit an app to the Windows Store.

What you need for this book

To follow the recipes in this book you will need a copy of Visual Studio 2012. Some of the features covered in the recipes may only be available in specific editions of Visual Studio, such as Ultimate.

If you wish to follow one of these recipes and you do not have the right edition, trial versions can be downloaded from the Microsoft website.

For any of the recipes that deal with Windows Store applications you will need to be using Windows 8 as your operating system.

Who this book is for

If you already know your way around previous versions of Visual Studio, if you are familiar with Microsoft development, and if you're looking to quickly get up to speed with the latest improvements in the 2012 incarnation of Microsoft's number one development tool then this book is for you.

Conventions

In this book, you will find a number of styles of text that distinguish between different kinds of information. Here are some examples of these styles, and an explanation of their meaning.

Code words in text are shown as follows: "Open the `VS2010_Web` solution and run the application."

Any command-line input or output is written as follows:

```
Get-Command *intelli*
```

New terms and **important words** are shown in bold. Words that you see on the screen, in menus or dialog boxes for example, appear in the text like this: "The **Preview Selected Items** button is a toggle button."

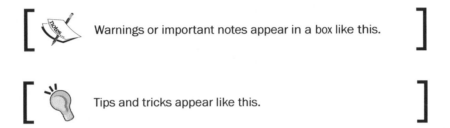

Warnings or important notes appear in a box like this.

Tips and tricks appear like this.

Reader feedback

Feedback from our readers is always welcome. Let us know what you think about this book—what you liked or may have disliked. Reader feedback is important for us to develop titles that you really get the most out of.

To send us general feedback, simply send an e-mail to `feedback@packtpub.com`, and mention the book title through the subject of your message.

If there is a topic that you have expertise in and you are interested in either writing or contributing to a book, see our author guide on `www.packtpub.com/authors`.

Customer support

Now that you are the proud owner of a Packt book, we have a number of things to help you to get the most from your purchase.

Downloading the example code

You can download the example code files for all Packt books you have purchased from your account at http://www.packtpub.com. If you purchased this book elsewhere, you can visit http://www.packtpub.com/support and register to have the files e-mailed directly to you.

Errata

Although we have taken every care to ensure the accuracy of our content, mistakes do happen. If you find a mistake in one of our books—maybe a mistake in the text or the code—we would be grateful if you would report this to us. By doing so, you can save other readers from frustration and help us improve subsequent versions of this book. If you find any errata, please report them by visiting http://www.packtpub.com/support, selecting your book, clicking on the **errata submission form** link, and entering the details of your errata. Once your errata are verified, your submission will be accepted and the errata will be uploaded to our website, or added to any list of existing errata, under the Errata section of that title.

Piracy

Piracy of copyright material on the Internet is an ongoing problem across all media. At Packt, we take the protection of our copyright and licenses very seriously. If you come across any illegal copies of our works, in any form, on the Internet, please provide us with the location address or website name immediately so that we can pursue a remedy.

Please contact us at copyright@packtpub.com with a link to the suspected pirated material.

We appreciate your help in protecting our authors, and our ability to bring you valuable content.

Questions

You can contact us at questions@packtpub.com if you are having a problem with any aspect of the book, and we will do our best to address it.

1
Discovering Visual Studio 2012

In this chapter, we will cover:

- ▸ Creating a new project
- ▸ Upgrading an existing solution
- ▸ Managing editor windows
- ▸ Finding Visual Studio commands
- ▸ Navigating and searching
- ▸ Searching your code
- ▸ Using the graphics tools

Introduction

When you open Visual Studio 2012 for the first time you're going to notice a few changes. We're going to start out by looking at some of the standard activities you will perform with Visual Studio in your normal development activities and in doing so discover a number of new and changed features in this powerful development tool.

These are tasks which are common to all developers regardless of the language they program in or the platform they are targeting.

Creating a new project

It might look the same as it did before, but there are a few changes when creating a new project. Let's create a new project and see what has changed.

Getting ready

Just make sure you have installed Visual Studio 2012 and you're all set to go.

How to do it...

1. Start Visual Studio 2012.

2. Choose the **File | New Project** menu option.

3. Examine the list of project types that are available and choose one that is of interest to you. If you're not sure what to choose, select **Visual C# | Class Library**.

4. Ensure that the project is targeting **.NET Framework 4.5** as shown in the following screenshot:

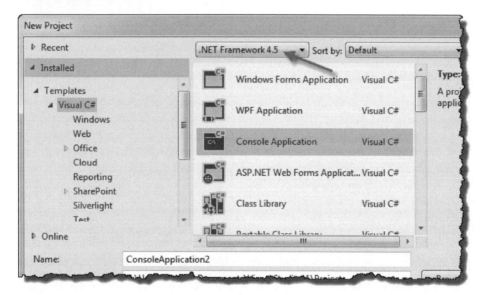

5. Enter a name of your choice for the project. If you feel lacking in creativity, take the default name and then click on **OK**.

6. The project is now created and you are ready to start writing code.

How it works...

On its own the project creation process in Visual Studio works exactly as it did in previous versions of Visual Studio, with the only difference being that you can now target .NET Framework 4.5.

There's more...

If that's all there was to it, it would hardly be worth talking about, however there are larger differences to be seen in the project creation area. Let's talk about them.

New project types and your development operating system

It's here that you will notice the first major change from Visual Studio 2010 and where you will see differences between Visual Studio 2012 running on Windows 8 versus a prior version of Windows.

The operating system you are using dictates whether you have access to the new **Windows Runtime (WinRT)** or not and thus whether you can write **Windows Store Applications** or not. On Windows 8 you will see a range of options for creating Windows Store Applications, whereas on Windows 7 and prior you will only see options for creating applications that do not use WinRT.

Portable class libraries

The **Portable Class Library** project template allows developers to create class library assemblies that can be referenced from not only standard .NET Framework applications, but also from Silverlight, Xbox 360 (XNA), and Windows Phone 7 projects.

This is at its most valuable when sharing service and data contracts or common domain classes between backend web services and frontend clients built using different technologies. For example, if previously you had a Silverlight application that used a set of web services running under ASP.NET then you would have to share code for those services by having separate projects for each runtime that looked exactly the same and used linked files to share the source.

Now all you have to do is move your common code into a single portable class library and add a reference to that portable library project from both your Silverlight project and your ASP.NET Web Application project.

Note that Portable Class Libraries are also available for Visual Studio 2010 using the Portable Library Tools extension from the Visual Studio Gallery (`http://visualstudiogallery.msdn.microsoft.com/b0e0b5e9-e138-410b-ad10-00cb3caf4981`).

Office projects

Visual Studio 2012 only provides project templates for Office 2010 projects. For Office 2007 projects you will need to continue using Visual Studio 2010.

Retired project templates

Visual Studio 2012 no longer has the Crystal Reports project template, nor does it feature Visual Studio Installer projects. If you are using Visual Studio Installer projects at the moment you will need to look at some different approaches. We cover some of the choices for creating installers in the *Appendix, Visual Studio Pot Pourri*

See also

▶ The *Creating a Windows Store app* recipe in *Chapter 2, Getting Started with Windows Store Applications*

Upgrading an existing solution

It's always nice to start a new project and if you've been working with legacy code for a while there's no better feeling! Unfortunately that feeling is often all too rare and we spend most of our time dealing with existing code with a long history.

All that legacy code is probably what's keeping you employed, so what you really want is to be able to open up that existing code in your shiny new copy of Visual Studio 2012 and bring the power of Visual Studio 2012 to bear on it, making life just that little bit easier for yourself.

One of the big changes in Visual Studio 2012 is that projects opened in Visual Studio 2012 are also backwards compatible with Visual Studio 2010 Service Pack 1 and we will see how that works. This process is called **round tripping**.

The good news for teams is that round tripping means they can gradually move from Visual Studio 2010 to Visual Studio 2012 as and when they are ready. They won't have the problems of the past where one team member checks in an upgraded solution file to source control, thus forcing the rest of the team to upgrade simply to continue working.

Getting ready

If you don't have any existing code you want to use you can use the sample Visual Studio 2010 solution we've prepared for you.

 The solution we will be using throughout this chapter is called VS2010_ Web and can be found at Chapter 1/VS2010_Web.

If you are going to use some of your existing code, ensure that the current code is in source control or that you have backed up the code.

In order to see the backwards compatibility in action you will need Visual Studio 2010 with Service Pack 1 installed on your machine.

How to do it...

1. Using either the **Open Project** link on the Visual Studio start page or the **File | Open | Project/Solution** menu select the `VS2010_Web` solution to start the conversion process.

2. Visual Studio will automatically migrate the solution and all the projects within it. When the process is complete you will be shown a migration report.

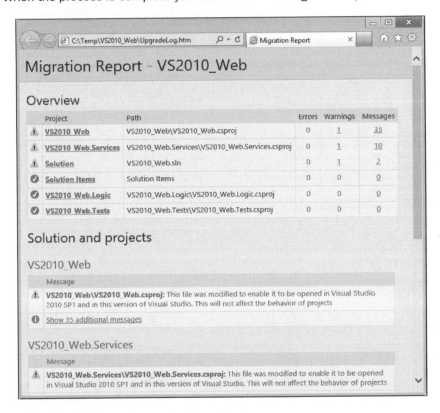

3. Close the report when you have finished looking at it.

4. From **Solution Explorer** open the `Default.aspx` file in the `VS2010_Web` project and change the **Welcome to ASP.NET!** text on the page to **Welcome to Visual Studio 2012!**.

5. Build and run the project to see that the application is working as expected.

6. Close Visual Studio 2012 and open Visual Studio 2010 with Service Pack 1.

7. Open the `VS2010_Web` solution and run the application.

8. You should see the web application appear, showing the updated message from Visual Studio 2012.

How it works...

The Visual Studio team worked with the various language and development product teams to ensure that project file formats would work consistently between Visual Studio 2010 and Visual Studio 2012. The first stage of these changes rolled out publicly with the release of Service Pack 1 for Visual Studio 2010, allowing Visual Studio 2010 to understand the new project formats.

When Visual Studio 2012 opens a Visual Studio 2010 project it will automatically upgrade the project format unless those changes will affect the ability to open the project in Visual Studio 2010. Any compatibility breaking changes will cause a dialog to be shown describing the changes and you can decide what action to take.

 Visual Studio 2012 will also upgrade projects created in Visual Studio 2008 and Visual Studio 2005, however round tripping of those projects is not supported. Likewise, the opening of a Visual Studio 2012 upgraded project in Visual Studio 2010 without Service Pack 1 is not supported.

There's more...

Not all project types will work with round tripping.

Visual Studio database projects

Visual Studio database projects aren't supported for round tripping. Visual Studio 2012 obsoleted Visual Studio database projects and replaced them with the new **SQL Server Data Tools (SSDT)** projects. When you open an old database project in Visual Studio 2012 you can upgrade it to an SSDT project. This project format also supports round tripping. However, if you wish to open an SSDT project in Visual Studio 2010 you will need to install the SQL Server Data Tools separately. You can download the tools from `http://msdn.microsoft.com/en-us/data/hh297027`.

ASP.NET MVC 2 projects

Visual Studio 2012 ships with support for both ASP.NET MVC 3 and ASP.NET MVC 4 projects. ASP.NET MVC 2 projects are not supported for round tripping in Visual Studio 2012 and therefore you will need to upgrade your MVC 2 projects to MVC 3 projects before opening them in Visual Studio 2012.

To help with the upgrade process you can use the ASP.NET MVC 3 Application Upgrader available from the ASP.NET Codeplex site at `http://aspnet.codeplex.com/releases/view/59008`.

Silverlight 3 and earlier

In a similar manner to ASP.NET MVC 2 projects, Silverlight 3 projects and prior will not be supported for round tripping with Visual Studio 2012. You will need to upgrade these projects to a later version of Silverlight first.

Visual Studio 2012 supports both Silverlight 4 and Silverlight 5 projects and you will be prompted for the version of Silverlight to use when you create a new project.

See also

▶ The *Using the new SQL Server Data Tools* recipe in *Appendix, Visual Studio Pot Pourri*

Managing editor windows

As you would expect, with a new Visual Studio version there comes a number of changes to how windows are managed. The changes that have been made have been done with the intention of reducing the clutter in your editing workspace and making the development experience one that is more focused on what you are doing.

Getting ready

Open either the VS2010_Web solution we have been using or use a solution of your choice.

Ensure that the **Solution Explorer** is open.

How to do it...

1. In **Solution Explorer** locate the Default.aspx.cs file in the VS2010_Web project and double-click it. The source file will open in the main window area as with previous versions of Visual Studio; however you will now notice that the document tab features a pin icon next to the tab namc as you can see in the following screenshot. You'll use that pin in just a few steps.

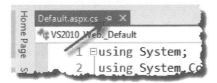

2. Using **Solution Explorer,** open both the About.aspx.cs and the Global.asax.cs files by double-clicking on them. You should now have three documents open with their tabs showing in the **tab well**.

3. Click on the **Default.aspx.cs** tab to select it and then click on the pin. The pin will change to point downwards indicating that the document is now pinned. Visual Studio 2012 will keep pinned tabs visible in the tab well even when you have so many open that Visual Studio starts hiding tabs. The pinned document tab will be moved to the left next to any other pinned documents you may have open.

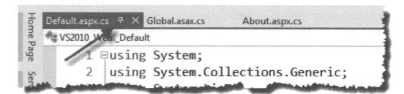

4. Right-click the **Global.asax.cs** document tab and click on **Close All But This** to close all open documents except for the one currently selected. This will include closing any pinned documents.

5. Reopen both the Default.aspx.cs and About.aspx.cs files that you closed by double-clicking on them in **Solution Explorer**.

6. One of the usability problems with document tabs in Visual Studio 2010 was that you could accidentally float documents by double-clicking a document tab. In Visual Studio 2012 this behavior has changed. Double-click on a document tab of your choice and notice how Visual Studio sets the focus to that tab instead of floating it. Much better!

7. Press *Ctrl+Shift+F* to open the **Find in Files** dialog. Enter **Class** in the **Find what** field and ensure **Look in** is set to **Solution**, then click on **Find All**.

8. In the **Find Results 1** window select a result from the ChangePassword.aspx file. The file will open in the preview tab, located on the right-hand side of the tab well.

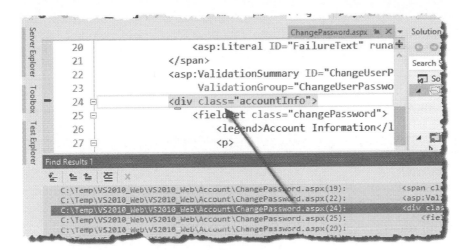

9. The preview tab shows the contents of the currently selected document if it is not already open. In the **Find Results 1** window select a result from `Login.aspx`. It will now be opened automatically in the preview tab and the `ChangePassword.aspx` document will be closed.

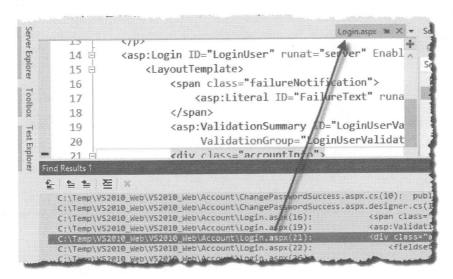

10. Assume you now want to keep `Login.aspx` open for a while. Either click the **Keep Open** icon in the tab or change the contents of the file. Any document in the preview tab that is changed is automatically promoted to a normal tab.

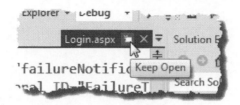

Visual Studio will move the document from the preview tab area into the main tab area. The color of the tab will also be changed from purple to blue indicating that the tab is now a normal document tab.

How it works...

Pinning documents works much like pinning does in any other part of Visual Studio and makes it very handy for keeping those documents you are working on regularly within easy reach, especially when you have many documents open at once.

The preview document tab is a great way to prevent tab clutter and becomes very useful when debugging deeply nested code. For example, say you have a section of code where a result you are expecting from a high-level method call is incorrect, and the source of the error actually is from a much lower-level method called at the end of a chain of four other intermediate methods, each from a different class. The odds are that you aren't really interested in those intermediate classes. Sure, you're happy to see those classes as you step through them on the way to the source of the problem, but you don't want to keep the documents open once you've moved past them. The preview tab means that during debugging, these class files are only opened temporarily, not permanently, helping you focus on just the code you are genuinely interested in and preventing the tab well filling up with documents you just aren't interested in.

There's more...

As always there are ways to customize the behavior of the document tabs in Visual Studio.

Single click preview in Solution Explorer

The preview tab isn't restricted to just the find results window. It can also be used from within **Solution Explorer**. If you activate the **Preview Selected Items** button in the **Solution Explorer** toolbar then every item you click on will be opened in the preview tab automatically.

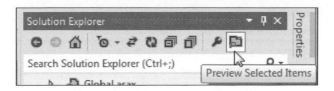

The **Preview Selected Items** button is a toggle button. If you want to disable the behavior then you only need to click on the button to deselect it and the preview behavior will be turned off.

Customizing tab and window behavior

Navigating to the **Tools | Options** menu in Visual Studio will show the following dialog box:

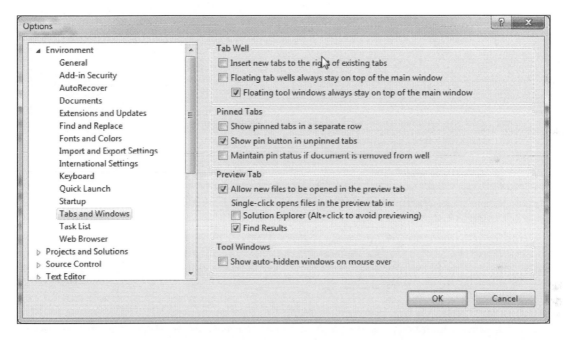

There are a number of options in here that let you control how the tabs behave. With Visual Studio 2010 Productivity Power Tools many developers found different ways to configure their tab well to get the experience they wanted, and while not everything from the power tools came across to the final Visual Studio 2012 product, a number of features most certainly did. Feel free to experiment with the **Tabs and Windows** settings to get Visual Studio working the way you like it most.

Finding Visual Studio commands

Visual Studio has a number of new commands in this release, combined with all the previous Visual Studio commands. Well, that makes for a lot of commands to try and keep in your head at once. Why take those brain cells where you stored all your sci-fi movie quotes and overwrite them with the intricate details of Visual Studio commands, when Visual Studio 2012 gives you an easy way to find the commands you're looking for with nothing more than a quick keystroke and a keyword or two? That's a win-win situation right there!

Let's see how this works.

Getting ready

Start Visual Studio 2012 and either open a project of your choice or the VS2010_Web project we've been using throughout this chapter.

How to do it...

1. Have a look at the top-right hand side of the Visual Studio editor window and you will see the new **Quick Launch** search box.

    For maximum speed the fastest developers try to minimize mouse usage and you're going to do the same for this recipe, so instead of clicking in the textbox to activate, press the shortcut key (*Ctrl+Q*). You will see that the **Quick Launch** box now activates and is waiting for your input.

2. Assume you want to open a file but you can't remember what the command is or where it might be hiding amongst all those menus. Yes, there's a really obvious **File** menu and it is the obvious place to look, but for the sake of the exercise pretend that you had almost no sleep last night, that you've just arrived at work today, that the coffee hasn't taken effect, your brain hasn't yet kicked into motion, and that you've forgotten where the open command lives.

    With the **Quick Launch** box active, enter the word open without pressing *Enter* and wait a moment for the search results to appear:

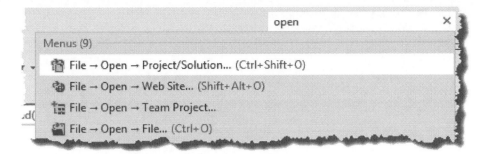

3. Take a look at the results. You'll see that not only are there the commands you might reasonably expect to see from the **File | Open** submenu, but also other commands you might not have realized existed, such as **Open Developer Account** (only if you are working in Windows 8). You can also see that the search results include Visual Studio options, not just the commands that are available.

4. Remembering that you are going through this recipe using only the keyboard, use the up and down cursor keys to navigate to a result of your choice and press *Enter* to execute that command.

5. You now need to open the `Default.aspx` page using just the Quick Launch tool and only with the keyboard. To do this you need to navigate to the `Default.aspx` file. Hit the **Quick Launch** shortcut (*Ctrl+Q*) and type in `nav` to see what commands are available:

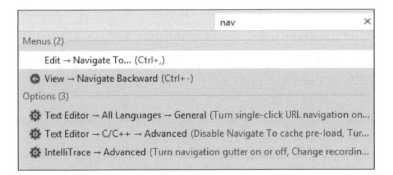

6. Press cursor down until the **Edit | Navigate To** entry is highlighted. Press *Enter* to activate the command.

7. In the resulting dialog box type `default` and wait momentarily for the search results to appear. Press cursor down until **Default.aspx** is highlighted and then hit *Enter*.

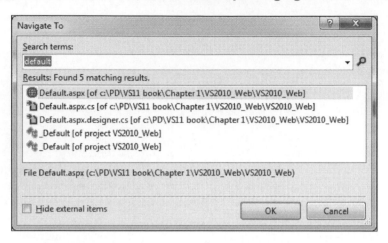

8. Now that you have the file open press the **Quick Launch** shortcut (*Ctrl+Q*) and type in **default**. In the search results you will not only see matching Visual Studio options, but also commands that perform different operations on the open `Default.aspx` file. That's pretty cool!

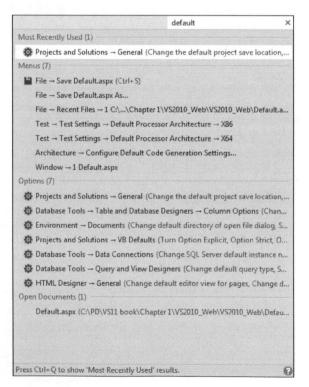

9. When there are a large number of results Visual Studio will show you a subset of those results based on what it deems to be the best matches for your search.

10. Use the **Quick Launch** control and enter the value debug. You will see a subset of all available results.

11. To see the full set of results simply press the **Quick Launch** shortcut again (*Ctrl+Q*). The expanded results are then shown.

How it works...

The Visual Studio team realized that the growing number of commands in Visual Studio was overwhelming for many people. Those people needed an easy way to quickly locate a command they were after without dredging through their memory cells for where that command might be hiding, or to waste time browsing through the various Visual Studio menus until they found it.

The **Quick Launch** search box is the recommended interface to find the commands you need, but don't use often enough to remember where they are.

There's more...

If you're a developer looking to improve your skills, be more productive, and maximize your use of the IDE, then knowing how to navigate your way around Visual Studio 2012 with nothing but the keyboard is a great goal to aim for. It minimizes the movement of your hand between the keyboard and the mouse which saves you time as well as gives you a greater sense of mastery over your tools. As a bonus, you'll also be able to impress your colleagues and dazzle them with your awesome Visual Studio skills!

If you find you use a command regularly, take the time to learn its specific shortcut key so you don't have to search for it every time you want to use it. For everything else, as long as you remember the name of the command or something close to it, you can use the **Quick Launch** control to find and execute that command without wasting time hunting through menus, and you won't have had to move your hands off the keyboard to do it.

Navigating and searching

As a code base grows it's important to be able to understand and find things quickly in your solution. The Solution Explorer we were used to in Visual Studio 2010 was good for being able to understand how files were organized into the various projects of a solution, but it didn't do much more than that.

With Visual Studio 2012, Microsoft has revisited **Solution Explorer** and given it an overhaul. It still contains all the functionality you know from the old **Solution Explorer** and adds to that a range of new features intended to make navigating and searching within your solution a more powerful, yet simpler experience.

Getting ready

Open the same `VS2010_Web` solution we have been using for the other recipes in this chapter or choose a solution of your own.

How to do it...

1. We'll begin with navigating through our solution. Locate the `Default.aspx` page in the `VS2010_Web` project and click the arrow next to it so that its contents are displayed. As you would expect there is a code behind file and a designer file.

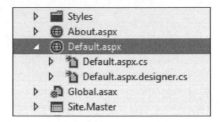

2. Look at the `Default.aspx.cs` file. You can see that there is a small arrow next to it just as there was for the `Default.aspx` page. Click on the arrow.

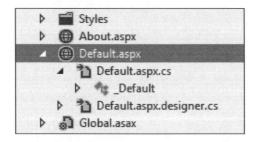

3. Visual Studio 2012 expands the file to show its contents and in the case of a code behind file those contents are the class definitions it contains. Classes have methods and properties in them, so click the arrow next to the `_Default` class to see the methods inside it. Since the `VS2010_Web` project is just a shell there is only an empty `Page_Load()` method as shown in the following screenshot:

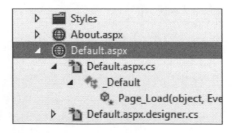

4. Now select the `IService1.cs` file from the `VS2010_Web.Services` project and expand it to see its contents. You will see that there is both an interface definition in this file (`IService1`) and a class definition (`CompositeType`) as shown in the following screenshot:

5. Right-click on the `IService1` interface and click **Derived Types** to see what classes implement this interface.

6. **Solution Explorer** will change views to show you the types that either implement this interface or inherit from it, as shown in the following screenshot. Click on the back button (showing the blue background) to return to the standard **Solution Explorer** view.

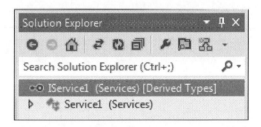

7. Right-click on the `IService1` interface and choose the **Is Used By** option to see where the interface is currently being used. As with the **Derived Types** option you will see **Solution Explorer** change context to only show the interface and where that interface is used in the solution, including line and column numbers.

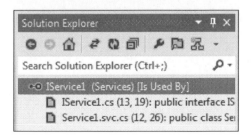

8. Return to the regular **Solution Explorer** view by clicking on the home button.

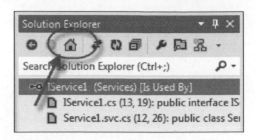

9. At this point you know how to navigate using **Solution Explorer** and you have already used the existing **Navigate To** feature from Visual Studio 2010 in the previous recipe (*Finding Visual Studio commands*) when opening a file. With the enhancements to **Solution Explorer** you can locate files in much the same way as with the **Navigate To** command, albeit with a slightly different user experience.

    Click in the **Search Solution Explorer** textbox at the top of **Solution Explorer** or use the default shortcut key of *Ctrl+;* (Ctrl+Semicolon).

10. Enter `serv` into the textbox and wait a moment for the search results to display. The results should look similar to the following screenshot. You can see not only the file names that match the search term, but also any matching references, classes, and methods.

How it works...

The **Navigate To** command from Visual Studio 2010 was a fantastic addition to Visual Studio. It had problems in large projects with many search matches since the location of a match was embedded in the result itself making it hard to locate the specific match you were after.

The new **Solution Explorer** search tool provides similar results to the **Navigate To** command, but having the location of a match represented in the tree view makes it very easy to quickly identify the specific match you are interested in.

There's more...

It's worth mentioning a few other things about searching within your solution.

Navigation behavior

Assuming you have the Preview tab enabled for **Solution Explorer** then as you navigate using **Solution Explorer** to various classes and methods you may have noticed that the document preview tab was updating and showing exactly where the selected class, method, or property is declared.

This makes it easy to see what the code is doing without the need to specifically open the file or scroll through a source file to see what code is actually inside a method, class, or property.

CSS, HTML, and JavaScript files

Even though it's possible to extract structure from CSS, HTML, and JavaScript files, **Solution Explorer** doesn't show the internal structure of these files. You can navigate to the source file but not to any of its contents.

See also

► The *Finding Visual Studio commands* recipe

Searching your code

You now know how to search within your solution for classes and methods and how to drill down into various items, but what if you are looking for a specific variable or piece of text in your code?

The **Find** tools in Visual Studio 2012 have been significantly revamped. It's time to use them and see what you can find.

Getting ready

Once again, open the same solution we have been using in the other recipes; either the VS2010_Web solution or a solution of your choosing.

How to do it...

1. Open the IService1.cs file from the VS2010_Web.Services project.

2. Ensure that focus is set to the code window, not **Solution Explorer**, and press *Ctrl+F*. This will trigger the new search tool as shown in the following screenshot. Alternatively you can access this from the menu using **Edit | Find and Replace | Quick Find**.

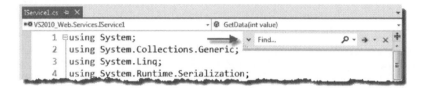

3. Enter the text service into the textbox. As you type you will notice that Visual Studio matches the search term against the code on the fly and all the matches are highlighted as shown in the following screenshot. This makes it very quick and easy to see if you have located the code you are looking for.

4. Since the search term has been matched multiple times it makes sense that you might want to quickly move between those matches. Press *F3* to move to the next match and press *Shift+F3* to move to the previous match.

5. Change the search term to serviceHost. Because there is no match in the current file the color of the border of the search box changes to red.

6. Given that you don't have a match in the current file it's worth expanding the scope of the search. Click on the expand icon on the left side of the search box and change the scope from **Current Document** to **Current Project**. When you do, you will notice that the red outline disappears indicating a match has been located.

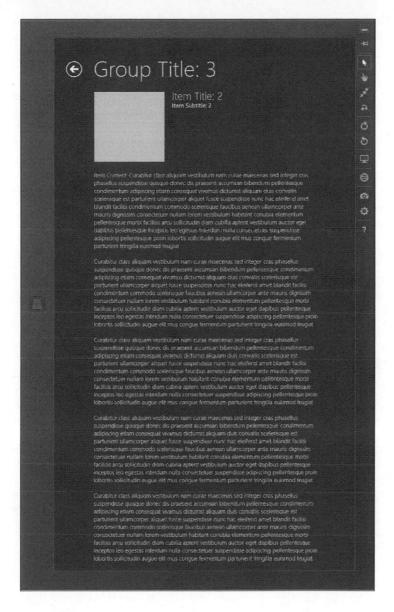

Click on the Rotate counterclockwise icon in the simulator to switch back to standard landscape mode.

13. Press the Windows icon on the simulator to bring up the start screen. Because the simulator is running a copy of your Windows environment you can start any of the apps that you have on your start screen.

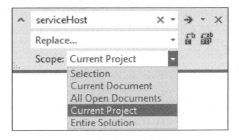

7. Press *F3* to find the next match. Note that the next matching file is opened as a normal document tab, not in the preview tab.

How it works...

By making the search dialog appear within the window that currently has focus, the user experience for both find and replace is much improved. It takes up only a small amount of space, it doesn't use a floating window, and the search box goes away when focus moves to a different window or document within Visual Studio, keeping the visual clutter low.

There's more...

When you clicked the button to expand the Quick Search tool window you may have noticed the option to replace text. This works as you would expect. Simply enter the text you want the search term replaced with and instead of pressing **Find Next** use the **Replace Next** button.

What happened to the old search dialog?

It's still there! Well, kind of. The changes in making search more context-specific mean that the **Quick Find** dialog is gone. If you have the focus somewhere other than a document tab and you press *Ctrl+F* or use the **Quick Find** command then the **Find and Replace** dialog will be shown with the **Find in Files** option selected. This is the same dialog box you will be familiar with from previous Visual Studio versions.

Can I use regular expressions?

This quick search dialog box doesn't support regular expression matches. Only the **Find and Replace** dialog box (via the **Find in Files** command) still supports regular expressions.

Using the graphics tools

The graphics tools in previous versions of Visual Studio might best be described as mediocre. However, in Visual Studio 2012 they have been revisited to provide some much needed updates.

Visual Studio 2012 in no way replaces a full featured graphics package, however if you just need to tweak an image or make some simple changes then Visual Studio can be very useful.

In this recipe, you'll create an image that you could use in the website project we've been using throughout this chapter.

Getting ready

Open the VS2010_Web project that we've been working with throughout this chapter.

How to do it...

1. Right-click on the VS2010_Web project and select **Add | New Folder**. Call the new folder Images.

2. With the Images folder selected, from the **File** menu choose **New File** or press *Ctrl+N*. From the **New File** dialog select **Graphics | PNG Image (.png)** and click on **Open**.

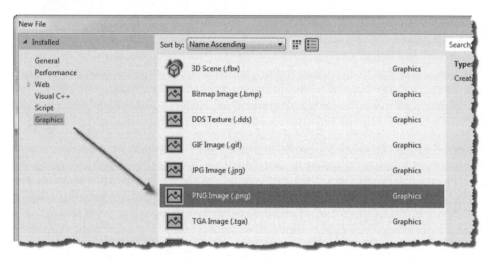

The new Visual Studio **Graphics Designer** will appear.

3. Save the image to the Images folder of your project using **File | Save As** with the default name of Image1.png.

4. In **Solution Explorer** turn on the **Show all files** option and locate the image you just saved to the Images folder. Include it in the project by right-clicking it and choosing the **Include In Project** option.

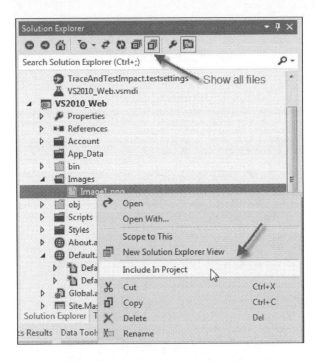

5.   Back in Graphics Designer you will see two new toolbars. One along the top of the image area and one along the side. For reference we will call these toolbars the **top toolbar** and the **side toolbar**.

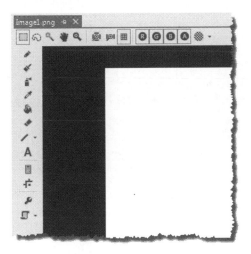

6. Select the Brush tool so you can draw on your wonderfully blank picture.

   To set the color of the brush, ensure the **Properties** panel is open. If it isn't it can be accessed by pressing *F4* or choosing **View | Properties Window**.

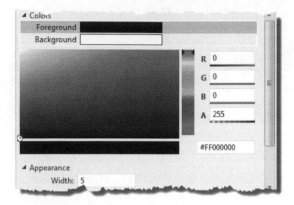

7. To select the brush thickness change the **Width** property of **Appearance** to a value of your choice, such as 10.

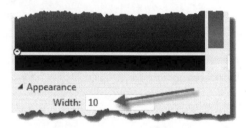

8. Now draw on the canvas and start creating your next masterpiece! Experiment with the other options in the toolbar to get a feel for what the graphics tool provides. Just make sure you produce something better than this horrible effort!!

How it works...

The new graphics designer is a DirectX accelerated design surface. You can alter the DirectX rendering output method to use software acceleration if, for example, you are using older hardware and are seeing graphics glitches. To switch, use the side toolbar and select **Advanced | Graphics Engines | Render with D3D11WARP**.

While the graphics editor is a much better editor that the previous resource editor, and even though DirectX acceleration means that the image editor can now work with very large, and complex images and a multitude of formats, it still isn't a match for a full featured graphics editing program. For advanced graphics needs, use a specialist tool.

There's more...

Visual Studio 2012 doesn't simply provide the same 2D image editing options of the past with a new interface; it now provides for some more advanced techniques specifically designed for those who need to produce visually rich applications such as games or information visualization tools.

MIP mapping support

MIP mapping is a technique used in video games for texture mapping 3D models. A single image file is structured to contain a high resolution texture as well as multiple versions of the same texture at lower levels of resolution. When the game is running, a texture of the appropriate resolution is extracted from the image file and applied to the 3D model based on the distance the model is from the camera. The further away the object, the lower the resolution chosen.

Visual Studio 2012 supports the editing of MIP map images using the new Graphics Designer.

3D Model support

You may have noticed when you were creating the PNG file that you also had the option to create a 3D scene.

Visual Studio 2012 supports the viewing, editing, and creating of **AutoDesk FBX** files, and also supports the viewing and editing (but not creating) of **OBJ** and **Collada DAE** files.

Pixel shaders

Visual Studio now supports the creating of **pixel shaders** in a visual manner using **DGSL (Directed Graph Shader Language)** as well as **HLSL shaders** using C++.

See also

▸ The *Creating a shader using DGSL* recipe in *Chapter 7, Unwrapping C++ Development*

▸ The *Creating and displaying a 3D model* recipe in *Chapter 7, Unwrapping C++ Development*

2
Getting Started with Windows Store Applications

In this chapter, we will cover:

- ► Creating a Windows Store app
- ► Adding a Windows Store item template to your app
- ► Using the Windows 8 simulator
- ► Defining capabilities and contracts
- ► Packaging your Windows Store app
- ► Validating your Windows Store app

Introduction

Microsoft Windows 8 features an all new look and feel with a redesigned Start menu and a fresh approach to desktop applications that will change the way people interact with Windows. These new desktop applications are known as Windows Store apps and are designed to be full screen, highly responsive, immersive, touch and cloud enabled applications. They are also designed to work on a wide variety of different form factors; supporting laptops, desktops, tablets, and anything else hardware manufacturers may create in the future. They are a radical departure from the way we have thought of applications in the past and will require fresh thinking from developers and designers alike. Windows Store apps should follow modern design principles of minimalism, focusing the user's attention on the information they are interested in and removing the distractions and visual noise that have traditionally been associated with Windows applications.

With Windows Store apps Microsoft is also ensuring that touch-enabled devices work just as well as the standard mouse and keyboard based desktops and laptops. Add to this that Microsoft wants Windows Store apps to be truly portable and we have before us a complete reimagining of the desktop application as we understand it.

There'll be no more install utilities or administrator access required in order to use an app. No more downloading software from the Web and wondering what kind of mess it will make on your machine or if it might have some malware with it. Instead people will purchase Windows Store apps from the Windows Store which can then be downloaded and run on whatever device they happen to be using at the time.

Apps listed in the Windows Store will have been verified by Microsoft as safe and as meeting standard app guidelines. This alleviates the trust problem people have with many Windows applications and follows the same approach Apple took with their iOS devices and the iTunes App Store as well as the Mac and the OS X app store.

It's one thing to have an app that you can download onto any device you're using but genuine portability requires that the data be portable as well. Microsoft has solved this problem by providing all Windows 8 users with **SkyDrive** storage space that Windows Store apps can use, making data available anywhere, anytime.

The introduction of Windows Store apps doesn't mean the traditional Windows desktop application is dead. Windows 8 supports the running of traditional desktop applications in **desktop mode**, with Visual Studio 2012 being a perfect example of one such application.

Now at this point, since you're a developer, what you are most likely interested in is not what's different with the user interface but what has been changed under the hood. What do you need to know to get started with Windows Store apps? The answer is the Windows Runtime.

Windows Runtime

The **Windows Runtime** is the API developers use for building Windows Store apps, sometimes called WinRT. Don't confuse it with **Windows RT**, the ARM version of Windows 8. The Windows Runtime API ensures apps can meet the design goals around portability, performance, and trust and with it Microsoft can also ensure Windows Store apps have zero ability to directly access the operating system preventing insecure and poor performing Windows API calls being made.

Windows Runtime abstracts away the underlying hardware, minimizes security risks, and prevents developers from making calls to long running methods that could freeze an app. It has also provided the opportunity to expand the technologies used to develop Windows Store apps.

Choosing the right development technology

When choosing the development technology it is critical to assess the development skill set of you and your team.

Until now, if you wanted to build traditional Windows desktop applications using Microsoft technologies, you were limited to using either C++ or .NET technologies. With the introduction of Windows Store apps, Microsoft has expanded the technology choice by adding JavaScript and HTML5 as a development choice.

If you and your team are comfortable with XAML development or you are a Java developer then your likely choice will be .NET.

C++ developers or those wanting to build DirectX apps will want to stick with C++.

Web developers, especially those with little knowledge of C++ or .NET, will love that they can build desktop apps with JavaScript and HTML5. For web developers Windows Runtime APIs are exposed via the provided WinJS libraries.

Creating a Windows Store app

This recipe will show you how to create a basic Windows Store app. For this recipe we're going to build it using HTML and JavaScript.

Getting ready

Ensure that you are running Windows 8. While Visual Studio 2012 can be installed on earlier versions of Windows, if you want to build Windows Store apps you must be using Windows 8. You cannot build a Windows Store app on Windows 7 or earlier.

Start Visual Studio 2012 and you're ready to go.

How to do it...

1. From the Visual Studio **File** menu select **New | Project**.

2. A dialog of available project templates will appear. From those templates select the **JavaScript | Windows Store | Grid App** template. A preview of the app layout will be shown in the details pane as shown in the following screenshot:

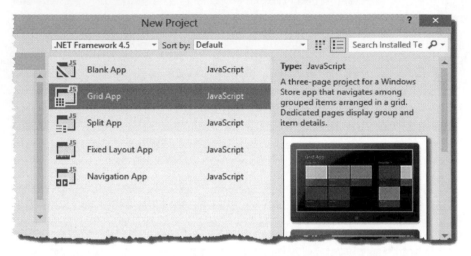

3. Leave the name as the default and click on **OK** to create the app.

4. The project will appear in **Solution Explorer** and the `default.js` file will be open in the document area.

5. Press *F5* to run the application in debug mode. Visual Studio will package and launch the app for you and you should see the app appear displaying a grouped collection of items that you can navigate.

6. Explore the app and when you are finished, close the app or switch back to Visual Studio and stop debugging.

How it works...

The steps for creating a Windows Store app are much the same as for creating any other type of application with the choice really being about the development technology to use and the style of app you are creating.

To create a **Split App** template or any of the other available Windows Store project types you would follow the same steps as outlined in the recipe. For each of the project types you will get a different result and a different starting point for your Windows Store development.

There's more...

There's a lot to consider when starting your first Windows Store apps. Fortunately Microsoft has made it fairly easy to choose the right starting point for the type of app you want to build.

What project type should I choose?

Each of the Windows Store project types, regardless of language, is described briefly here so that you can determine what template would make a good starting point for your development efforts.

Blank App

The **Blank App** template is exactly what you would expect. It is an empty shell ready for you to start coding with.

Grid App

The **Grid App** template is designed to show a summarized view of a data source in a grid layout. The project template includes a sample data source so that you can quickly get a feel of how the app works. Running the app without changes shows the grid summary page as shown in the following screenshot:

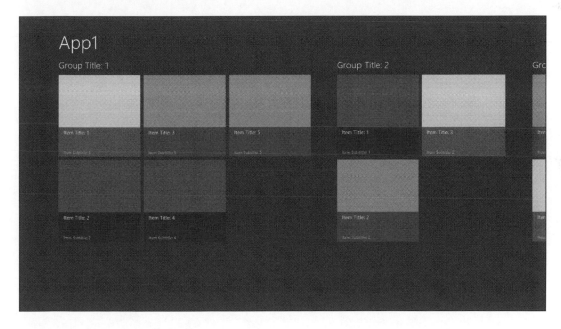

Note how the data is grouped into collections and how the individual items in each collection are shown with a placeholder for an image thumbnail and a few lines of text to describe the item. Selecting one of the items will navigate to the detail view of that item as shown in the following screenshot:

The template also includes a collection level summary page, shown when the back button next to the collection name is clicked or touched. This view is shown in the following screenshot:

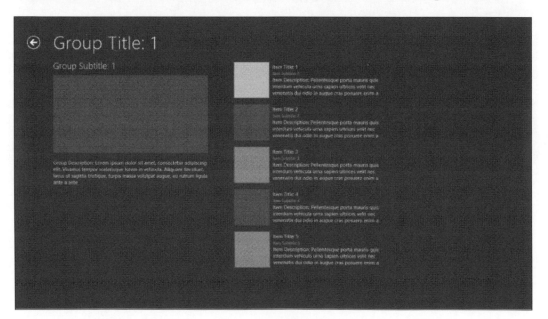

Split App

The **Split App** template is an alternative to the Grid App template, though it is still based around the concept of consuming data grouped into collections.

Just like the **Grid App** template, the **Split App** template provides a ready to run app so you can see how it functions.

Launching the app shows a home page very similar to the **Grid App** template, but it has a very different group level page where the items in the collection are displayed in a column on the left side of the screen and the details of the selected item are shown on the right as seen in the following screenshot:

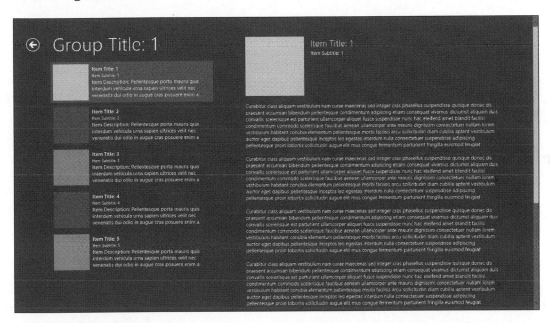

Fixed Layout App

The **Fixed Layout App** template is only available when using JavaScript and provides a basic app featuring a minimal splash screen and a skeleton HTML file, with all the necessary WinJS references ready for you to start building your app.

Navigation App

The **Navigation App** template is the same as the **Fixed Layout App** template with the inclusion of an **AppBar** and basic navigation controls ready for you to use. If you run the app without any changes you will see a splash screen followed by a very minimalist page ready for your creativity to be applied to it.

Class Library

The **Class Library** project creates a managed assembly for your app logic that is automatically set to use the .NET Framework 4.5 Windows Store profile.

Unit Test Library

The **Unit Test Library** project template creates an **MSTest** or **CppUnit** based test assembly for unit testing your code.

DLL (Windows Store apps)

The **DLL (Windows Store apps)** template is a C++ project template for creating a DLL in which you can write your app logic. It contains all the include files you would expect for building a DLL for a Windows Store app as well as a skeleton `DllMain` method ready for you to implement.

Static Library (Windows Store apps)

The **Static Library** template is just as the sticker on the box says. A simple skeleton with the include files you need for building a static library for use in a C++ Windows Store app.

Windows Runtime Component

Similar to the Class Library in .NET **Windows Runtime Component** is a project template for creating a DLL using C++ and targeting Windows Runtime so that the logic can also be used in .NET or HTML5 Windows Store apps.

Direct2D App (XAML) and Direct3D App

The **Direct2D App (XAML)** and the **Direct3D App** templates are for C++ apps using the **DirectX** runtime for high performance graphics and audio processing. Typically this will be for Windows Store game development though they could also be used for many business apps such as medical imaging and audio processing.

At this stage DirectX is the only choice for Windows Store game development. **XNA** is not supported for Windows Store apps and XNA applications on Windows 8 will only run as Windows desktop applications. For clarity, XNA is still the technology of choice for Xbox Live Arcade and Windows Phone 7 games.

Technology choice impacts available project templates

Given that there are a lot of project templates available and there is also more choice in development technologies it is important to be clear about which project templates are available for which technology.

The following table indicates which app types are available for each technology choice:

	JavaScript/HTML	.NET	C++
Blank App	Y	Y	Y
Grid App	Y	Y	Y
Split App	Y	Y	Y
Fixed Layout App	Y		
Navigation App	Y		
Class Library		Y	
Unit Test Library		Y	Y
Windows Runtime Component		Y	Y
DLL			Y
Static Library			Y
Direct 2D/3D App			Y

.NET projects and the Windows Store apps profile

When developing projects in Visual Basic or C# you will be working with .NET Framework 4.5 using the Windows Store profile. You will not have access to all of the .NET Framework methods and libraries that you are used to when building traditional Windows desktop or web applications, and if you look in your project references instead of the usual references you will see a reference to **.NET for Windows Store apps**.

This change is largely because much of the functionality .NET historically provided has now been incorporated directly into Windows Runtime. .NET is now just a supplement to the Windows Runtime. Additionally, the .NET Windows Store profile removes classes and methods that aren't applicable for Windows Store apps, which results in a dramatically smaller application footprint.

Language interoperability

JavaScript Windows Store apps can call functionality written in either C++ or .NET when that functionality is contained in libraries or DLLs that expose WinMD metadata. Unfortunately the reverse is not the case; .NET and C++ apps cannot call functionality contained in JavaScript libraries.

C++ Windows Store apps can however call functionality in .NET WinMD assemblies (that is, created using the **Windows Runtime Component** project type) and .NET code can call C++ Windows Runtime components as well. The good news here is that there is no longer a need to use **COM Interop** for any of these cross language calls, making language interoperability much, much simpler when developing Windows Store apps than it is for Windows desktop applications.

Adding a Windows Store item template to your app

Unless you're building a Hello World app you're probably going to want to add more code files and assets to your project than are provided with the standard project templates.

Because Microsoft wants Windows Store apps to not only offer great functionality, but to also meet the Windows Store design principles, they have provided a number of ready-made item templates for you to use as part of your development efforts. User interface item templates come with a common look and feel and subtle animations so your app behaves like other Windows Store apps. Contract templates provide you with boiler plate code and UI for building Windows 8 Contract support into your app.

In this recipe you'll see how to use an item template to add functionality to a Windows Store app.

Getting ready

Create a new blank Windows Store app using C# by following the steps in the *Creating a Windows Store app* recipe.

How to do it...

1. Right-click your project and select **Add | New Item**.
2. Select **Windows Store** from the left-hand panel and choose the **Items Page** template as shown in this screenshot:

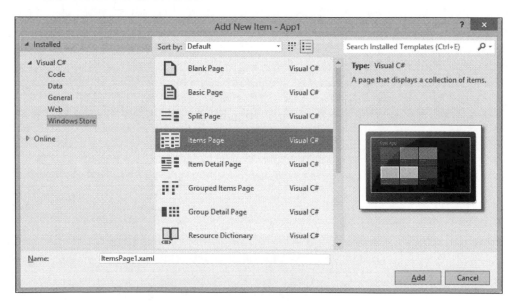

3. Leave the name of the item as the default and click on the **Add** button. The new item will be added to your project ready for you to start working on.

4. You will be prompted to add files to your project to resolve dependencies in Common namespace. Click on **Yes** in the dialog box to continue.

5. When the item page appears the XAML will be displayed but the designer will be showing a message that the code hasn't yet been compiled. Build the project to ensure that the designer can display correctly.

6. Add a new class to the project named `DataClass` and define it as follows, just remember to adjust the `using` statement to reflect your application's name.

```
using App2.Common;

namespace App2
{
    public class DataClass : BindableBase
    {
        public string Title { get; set; }
        public string Subtitle { get; set; }
    }
}
```

7. Navigate to `ItemPage1.xaml.cs` and change the body of the `LoadState()` method to the following:

```
protected override void LoadState(Object navigationParameter,
{
    var list = new List<DataClass>(){
        new DataClass(){Title = "One",Subtitle="First Item"},
        new DataClass(){Title = "Two",Subtitle="Second Item"}
    };

    this.DefaultViewModel["Items"] = list;
}
```

8. In the `App.xaml.cs` file locate the `OnLaunched` method and the section where `rootFrame` is defined (line 58). Change the type used in the `Navigate` method from `MainPage` to `ItemsPage1` as shown in the following screenshot:

```
var rootFrame = new Frame();
if (!rootFrame.Navigate(typeof(ItemsPage1)))
{
    throw new Exception("Failed to create initial page");
}
```

9. Press *F5* to debug and run the application. Your item list should now appear as shown in the following screenshot:

How it works...

Using an item template to add functionality to an app is generally the same as in previous versions of Visual Studio. The additional dialog to generate the Common namespaces only appears for the first item template you add to your project.

For the UI item templates, support is provided for the various views that Windows Store apps need to support, specifically the **Full**, **Fill**, **Snapped**, and **Portrait** states.

The `DataTemplate` definitions for each item displayed can be found in the `Common\StandardStyles.xaml` file and is where the property names of the item specific data binding can be found.

There's more...

Of course you aren't limited to just the **Items Page** template. You can use any of the other available templates to add functionality to your app.

What are the other Windows Store item templates?

The following list describes what will be added for each of the new **Windows Store** item templates.

Blank Page

The **Blank Page** item template gives you an empty blank page. What did you expect?

Basic Page

The **Basic Page** item template is the **Blank Page** item template with added layout awareness, a title, and a back button to give you a starting point for creating your own layouts.

Split Page

The **Split Page** item template displays a vertical list of items on the left and the details of the selected item on the right.

Items Page

The **Items Page** item template displays a flat view of an object collection, as you saw in the recipe.

Item Detail Page

The **Item Detail Page** item template shows a detailed view of a single item using a **FlipView** control. It also provides navigation options for moving to the next or previous item in the collection.

Grouped Items Page

The **Grouped Items Page** item template adds a summarized view of items arranged into groups.

Group Detail Page

The **Group Detail Page** item template provides a panel for displaying the items from a single group in a collection, and summary views of the items in the group.

File Open Picker Contract

The **File Open Picker Contract** item template adds a UI for displaying file selection choices to the user via the Windows 8 file picker. The code behind for the item template includes the `Activate` method with the `FileOpenPickerActivatedEventArgs` parameter you can query to determine what to show. You will also need to populate the `FileOpenPickerUI` property of this parameter to return selections to the calling app.

Search Contract

The **Search Contract** item template provides a standard page for displaying search results initiated from the Windows 8 search charm and includes the criteria and filters used in that search.

Share Target Contract

The **Share Target Contract** item template adds a standard page for selecting items to share via the Windows 8 share contract.

Language impacts item template options

Just like the project templates you saw in the *Creating a Windows Store app* recipe, the development technology you choose limits the Windows Store item templates available for use. The following table indicates which items are available for each technology choice in the Windows Store item category:

	.NET	JavaScript	C++
Blank Page	Y		Y
Basic Page	Y		Y
Split Page	Y		Y
Items Page	Y		Y
Item Detail Page	Y		Y
Grouped Items Page	Y		Y
Group Detail Page	Y		Y
File Open Picker Contract	Y	Y	Y
Search Contract	Y	Y	Y
Share Target Contract	Y	Y	Y

See also

▸ The *Creating a Windows Store app* recipe

Using the Windows 8 simulator

You may recall that one of the design goals of Windows Store apps was that they should run equally well on a multitude of devices, including tablets and other touch-enabled devices and they should also support a number of different views such as the **Snapped** and **Full** views.

I'm not sure about you, but most developers I know use powerful desktops or high-end laptops for developing software and at this point in time those machines aren't typically equipped with touch input or gyroscopes. Well, not yet anyway.

Microsoft realized that this would likely be the case and have included with Visual Studio 2012 a **Windows 8 Simulator** that can be used to test your Windows Store apps without the need of a second physical machine to deploy to.

The simulator is similar in concept to the Microsoft Windows Phone 7 emulator used in developing Windows Phone 7 software. Let's have a look at how we make use of the simulator.

Getting ready

Create a new C# Windows Store Split app and name it SplitApp. You can use the information from the *Creating a Windows Store app* recipe if you need a refresher on how to do this.

How to do it...

1. Go to the **Properties** page of the SplitApp project.

2. Select the **Debug** tab and change the target machine to **Simulator** as shown in the following screenshot:

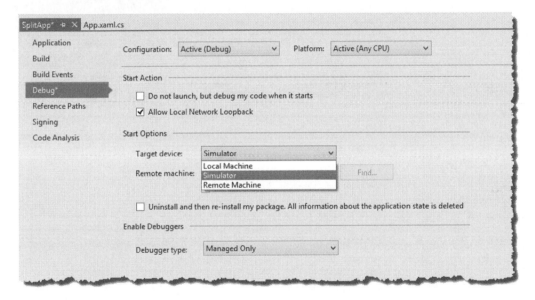

3. Start debugging the app by either pressing *F5* or selecting the **Debug | Start Debugging** menu option.

4. Visual Studio will start the Windows 8 Simulator and launch the app for you as shown in the following screenshot:

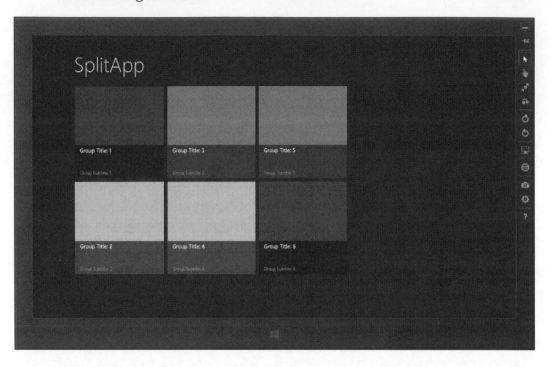

5. On the right-hand side of the simulator are a number of icons that control the simulator's behavior. By default, the simulator starts in mouse mode so you can navigate within the app using the keyboard and mouse.

For reference the toolbar icon functions are, from top to bottom: Minimize, Always on top, Mouse mode, Basic touch mode, Pinch/zoom touch mode, Rotation touch mode, Rotate clockwise, Rotate counterclockwise, Change resolution, Set location, Copy screenshot, Screenshot settings, and Help.

6. Click on the **Group Title: 3** group and then the **Item Title: 3** item from the list on the left and move the mouse over the detail section on the right. You should see the contents of the details panel change and a scroll bar should appear as shown in the following screenshot:

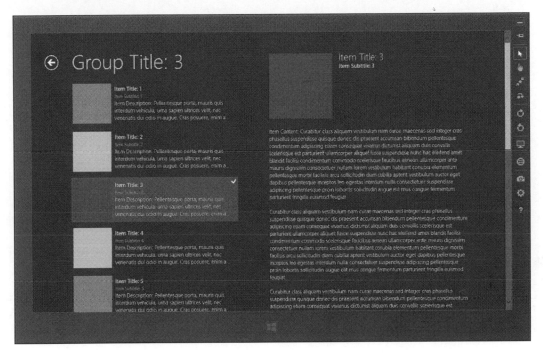

7. Switch to the Basic touch mode by selecting the icon on the simulator toolbar.

8. As you move your mouse over the simulator you will see that the cursor has now changed to be a small crosshairs in a circle icon. Click on the second item in the collection to select it.

9. Move the mouse over the details pane and simulate an upwards swipe by left-clicking and dragging upward with your mouse to scroll the details pane.

10. As you do, you should see the pointer change to a partially filled in circle indicating that you are touching the screen, and the contents of the pane should scroll as you move the mouse. This is illustrated in the following screenshot:

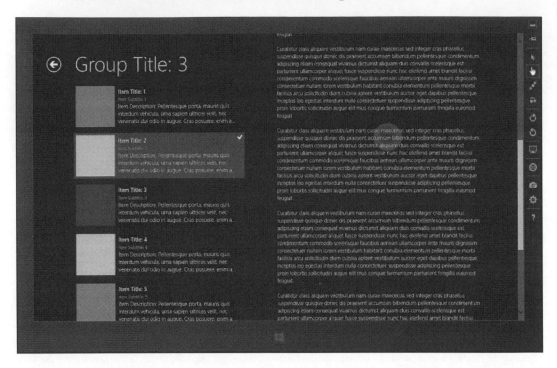

11. So far so good. Now it's time to flip the simulator to portrait mode. Click on the Rotate clockwise icon.

12. The simulator should now look as it does in the following screenshot with the layout of the content adapting as the device is rotated:

14. When the simulator has focus it will capture the keyboard and handle key combinations such as *Alt+Tab* or *Alt+F4*. Close the simulator using *Ctrl+Alt+F4*.

15. Back in Visual Studio open the `SplitPage.xaml.cs` file and locate the `Page_OrientationChanged()` method.

16. Set a breakpoint in the `ItemListView_SelectionChanged()` method either by pressing *F9* or clicking in the gutter to the left of the code. This should be line 128.

```
void ItemListView_SelectionChanged(object sender, SelectionChangedEventArgs e)
{
    // Invalidate the view state when logical page navigation is in effect, as a change
    // in selection may cause a corresponding change in the current logical page.  When
    // an item is selected this has the effect of changing from displaying the item list
    // to showing the selected item's details.  When the selection is cleared this has the
    // opposite effect.
    if (this.UsingLogicalPageNavigation()) this.InvalidateVisualState();
}
```

17. Start debugging the app again by pressing *F5*.

18. When the application starts, select a group to display. The breakpoint will be hit and you could at this point step through the code to understand how it works.

How it works...

The Windows 8 simulator is actually connecting to your local machine via a remote desktop connection and is why the Start screen in the simulator looks the same as the Start screen on your Windows 8 development machine and why you are signed in automatically.

Because it's a remote desktop connection running on the local machine the debugger is simply connecting to a local process running in a different session. If you open the **Attach to Process** window via the **Debug | Attach to Process** menu you can see the details of the process Visual Studio has connected to. The following screenshot highlights the details of the running `splitapp.exe` and shows that it is in session 2, which is the Windows 8 Simulator session.

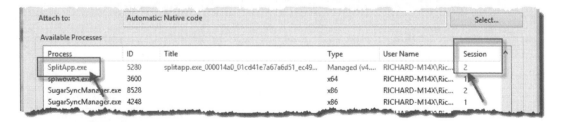

There's more...

There are a few more things to note about the simulator that we didn't touch on in the recipe.

Resolution and resizing

You can adjust the resolution the simulator is running at, allowing you to experience your app at different predefined resolutions and device sizes.

Along with changing the resolution you can also change the onscreen display size of the simulator by dragging the bottom-right hand corner of the simulator just like a normal desktop window. This can help if you are simulating a device on a high resolution desktop and you have the screen real estate to spare. Why stare at those tiny fonts? Use those pixels and save your eyes!

Remote debugging

You may have noticed that when you set the debug option for using the simulator that there was also a **Remote Machine** option.

Remote debugging is much simpler under Visual Studio 2012 developing Windows Store apps than has previously been the case for Windows desktop apps. For the **Remote Machine** option to work you need to have the **Remote Debugging Monitor** running on the remote machine, the firewall needs to allow connections and you need a reasonable network connection between the two machines.

On your development machine you simply specify the machine name of the remote machine you are targeting and start debugging. Visual Studio connects to the remote machine, prompts for credentials if required, deploys the app, and connects the remote debugging monitor for you.

From that point forward the debug experience is almost the same as if it were a local process. As long as you have a stable network connection you should find the experience very straightforward.

Location settings

The simulator lets you enter a simulated location that incorporates not only **Latitude** and **Longitude** but also the **Altitude** and an **Error radius** so that you can test location-aware apps on hardware that don't support GPS or location awareness.

If you have a location-aware device then you can turn off the simulated values and use the values of the device itself.

Taking screenshots

When you want to take screenshots of your Windows Store apps, for creating your store listing for example, then you can do so via the simulator. Simply click on the **Copy screenshot** button on the toolbar and the screenshot will be placed on the clipboard and optionally in a file on your hard drive. You can control this behavior using the **Screenshot settings** button on the toolbar.

See also

▸   The *Creating a Windows Store app* recipe

Defining capabilities and contracts

Windows 8 provides Windows Store apps with the ability to communicate with any other app on the computer without prior knowledge of what those apps might be through a concept called Contracts. A **Contract** is an operating system level interface that consumers or providers of information implement. The operating system then keeps track of which apps support which contracts and coordinates the information between apps using those contracts.

Window 8, as part of its focus on improving the trust level in the apps it runs, expects Windows Store apps to communicate the capabilities they need. A **Capability** is a permission or access right that a Windows Store app requires for it to run correctly, for example an app that requires Internet access or local network permissions. There are a range of capabilities that the operating system can provide to Windows Store apps. An app that doesn't request capabilities from the operating system will be provided minimum level access, meaning that it will run in its isolated process space with no access to any external resources at all.

Similarly an app may have one or more Declarations. A **Declaration** is an attribute of the app that provides extra information the operating system can use to further integrate the app into the standard operating system experience. For instance an app declaring the file picker contract is telling the operating system that it can be a source of files when the user is using a file picker.

In this recipe you will add a contract declaration and adjust the capabilities of a Windows Store app.

Getting ready

Open the `SplitApp` you created in the previous recipe, *Using the Windows 8 simulator*.

How to do it...

1. Open the `Package.appxmanifest` file from **Solution Explorer**. The manifest file will open up in the main document window as shown in the following screenshot:

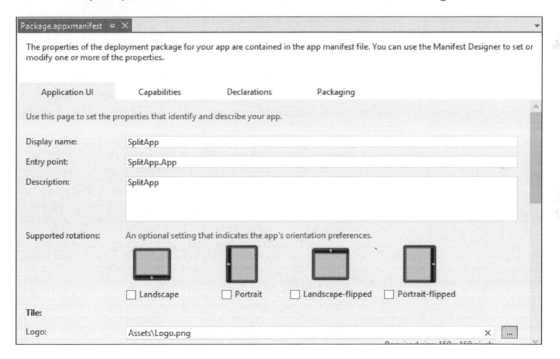

2. Select the **Capabilities** tab:

```
Package.appxmanifest   ⊡ ✕

The properties of the deployment package for your app are contained in the app manifest file. You can

  Application UI        Capabilities        Declarations        Packaging

Use this page to specify system features or devices that your app can use.

Capabilities:                              Description:
  ☐ Documents Library Access               Enables adding, changing, or deleting files in the d
  ☐ Enterprise Authentication              types that are defined by the file type association ha
                                           cannot access document libraries on HomeGroup
  ☐ Home or Work Networking
  ☐ Internet (Client & Server)             More information
  ☑ Internet (Client)
  ☐ Location
  ☐ Microphone
  ☐ Music Library
  ☐ Pictures Library Access
  ☐ Proximity
  ☐ Removable Storage
  ☐ Shared User-Certificates
  ☐ Text Messaging
  ☐ Videos Library Access
  ☐ Webcam
```

3. You should only declare the capabilities you actually need and the `SplitApp` does not require any **Internet (Client)** access. Deselect this capability.

4. Select the **Declarations** tab.

5. From the **Available Declarations** drop down select **Search** and then click on the **Add** button:

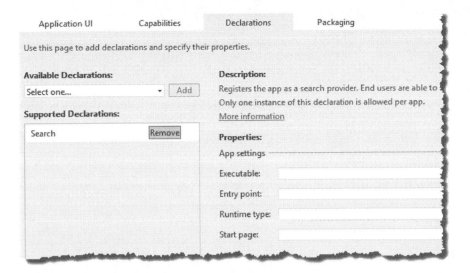

6. At this point you are registering the `SplitApp` as a search target so that users can search the app from anywhere in the operating system using the search charm. **RuntimeType** indicates to the operating system the type of items the app provides and **StartPage** indicates what page the app should use to display a selected search result. You're not going to implement a search provider as part of this recipe so for now just click on the **Remove** button next to **Search** in the **Supported Declarations** section.

How it works...

One of the design goals for Windows Store apps is that they should be portable, meaning that it should be easy to download them from the Windows Store and run them on any computer the user desires without needing any special permissions. For this to work a Windows Store app cannot use an installer the way a Windows desktop application does. Installers require administrator permission to execute, generally access the registry, ask the user what parts of the application should be installed, and decide how and where the app should be located on disk, all of which prevents portability. In the case of Windows Store apps it's Windows itself that determines this behavior and it does so by inspecting the **App Manifest** that is provided with each app.

The App Manifest is a critical file for any Windows Store app and you need to pay attention to it. It contains all of the declarative information to inform Windows of the capabilities it needs as well as the contracts that it satisfies.

There's more...

It's great that there are so many capabilities and contracts you can declare, but instead of describing all of the possible contracts that you can implement, let's have a look at the ones you are most likely to consider for your apps.

Contracts

The following details the various contracts that you can declare for your app.

Contact Picker

Let's say your app exposes information from your company address book. The **Contact Picker** contract will let other apps wanting to retrieve contact information use your app as a source of contact details.

File Open Picker

An app may want to include, for example, a picture in an e-mail. Your app can provide images for that app to use by implementing the **File Picker** contract. The **SkyDrive** app provided with Windows implements the File Picker contract, which is why it is listed as a source when you browse for a **Lock Screen** picture from the **PC settings** app, as shown in the following screenshot:

Search

The **Search** contract, as we saw in our recipe, allows the end user to search for information from within your program. Any program that implements the Search contract item template will be listed as a search source when the Search charm is used. For example, as shown in the following screenshot, the **Weather** app implements the Search contract:

File Type Associations

If your app is going to be accessing files in the **Documents Library** you will need to specify the extensions of the files that you will be accessing and you must select the **Documents Library Access** capability in the **Declarations** tab. Only files with these extensions will be available for your app.

Share Target

The **Share Target** contract is used when you want to share something with someone else. For example, sharing web addresses on Twitter or Facebook, or sharing a picture with friends. The contract definition lets you determine what type of files or data can be shared (for example, jpg files, e-mail addresses, and URLs).

This contract is a little different to the previous ones you've seen. The contract is indicating the app is a consumer of the shared information, not a source as with the other contracts.

Capabilities

As with the contracts, not all capabilities are going to be of interest for most developers. The following are some of the more important ones that you should be aware of.

Internet (Client)

The **Internet (Client)** capability lets Windows know that your app will be making requests to Internet-based resources but it will not be receiving any connections. It is for outbound connections on public networks only.

Given most Windows Store apps are expected to have some level of Internet connectivity this is enabled by default in the project templates.

Internet (Client & Server)

The **Internet (Client & Server)** capability informs Windows that your app will not only request data but will also be serving data and can accept inbound connections.

Even if you specify this capability you cannot accept inbound connections on critical ports. Specifying this capability means you do not need to specify the **Internet (Client)** capability, and if you do it will have no effect.

Home or Work Networking

Windows 8 maintains the concept of network profiles for your machine and the Home and Work networks are considered to be private networks with separate security profiles from the public Internet. The **Home or Work Networking** capability allows you to make both inbound and outbound connections on these trusted networks.

As with the **Internet (Client & Server)** capability, you cannot accept connections on critical ports.

Library access

Windows Store apps have limited access to the filesystem and must request access as part of their capabilities. The **Documents Library Access**, **Music Library Access**, **Pictures Library Access**, and **Videos Library Access** capabilities must be selected in order to access files in each of those locations.

When accessing a library only files with extensions listed in the **File Type Association** contract will be available.

Packaging your Windows Store app

For Windows 8 to correctly load and run a Windows Store app it must be packaged in a particular format. The information contained in the package includes the capabilities and contracts that your app uses as well as information on the app user tile, the splash screen, and more.

This recipe will show you what you need to do to package your Windows Store app so that it is ready for the world to use.

Getting ready

Open the SplitApp that you created in the *Using the Windows 8 simulator* recipe.

How to do it...

1. Open the `Package.appxmanifest` file from **Solution Explorer**.

2. Examine the fields in the **Application UI** tab. Add a space to the **Display Name** field so that it reads as **Split App** instead of `SplitApp`.

3. Add a useful description in the **Description** field. For example: **A sample app using the Split layout**.

4. In the **Tile** section confirm the **Show Name** field is set to **All Logos**. This will make the name of the app appear on the **Tile** on the Windows Start screen.

5. In the **Packaging** tab adjust the **Package Display Name** to include a space so that the package name is **Split App**.

6. Save your changes to the manifest file.

7. Build the solution.

8. In **Solution Explorer** select the `SplitApp` project and then click on the **Show All Files** icon as shown in the following screenshot:

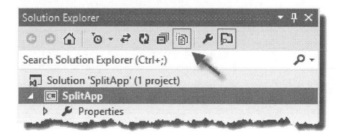

9. Navigate to the `bin\Debug` folder so that you can see the output from the build. This is the output that will be uploaded to the Windows store when you publish your app. It should look something like the following following screenshot:

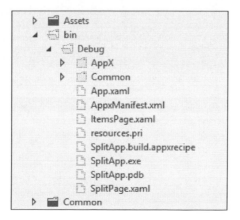

10. In Visual Studio, right-click on the solution in **Solution Explorer** and select **Deploy Solution** as shown in the following screenshot. This will deploy the **Split App** template to your local machine ready for use.

11. Press the Windows key to bring up the Start screen and scroll to the far right. You should see an icon for the **Split App** template as shown in the following screenshot:

12. Deploying locally is great, but if you want to test your app on another machine you will need to create a package. Right-click on the `SplitApp` project in **Solution Explorer** and select the **Store | Create App Package** option from the context menu

13. Select **No** when asked to build a package for the Windows Store and click on **Next**. Packaging for the Windows Store is discussed in the *Appendix, Visual Studio Pot Pourri*.

14. Leave all the default values as they are and click on **Create**.

Wait until the package creation process completes and click on **OK** to dismiss the notification dialog.

15. Once the package finishes building, refresh **Solution Explorer** and you should now see an **AppPackages** folder appear that contains the package ready for local deployment as shown in the following screenshot:

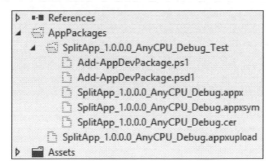

How it works...

You may notice in the `bin\Debug` folder that there are a few extra files generated, namely the `resources.pri`, `AppxManifest.xml`, and `SplitApp.build.appxrecipe` files.

The `AppxManifest.xml` file is simply a renamed copy of the `package.appxmanifest` file.

The `resources.pri` file contains the app resources in binary format and the `SplitApp.build.appxrecipe` file is used for incremental builds of the package so that each time the package is rebuilt, the package version number is automatically incremented.

In the `AppPackages` folder there is an `*.appxupload` file which is a zip archive containing the app and any debug symbols, and there is a layout folder with a name based on the app, the CPU type, and so forth. In this case it is called `SplitApp_1.0.0.0.AnyCPU_Debug_Test`.

Doing a deployment of the app to a test machine is simply a matter of copying the layout folder to the test machine and running the `Add-AppDevPackage.ps1` PowerShell script from that folder.

There's more...

There are a few other things to be aware of when packaging your app.

Package signing

Packages need to be signed in order to be uploaded to the Windows Store. When developing locally, Visual Studio uses a temporary certificate. However deploying to the Windows Store will require a certificate issued by the store.

Tile notifications

If you want your app to use tile notifications you need to supply a **Wide Logo** in the **Tile** section of the **App UI** tab as notifications only apply to Start screen tiles in wide mode.

See also

▸ The *Submitting apps to the Windows Store* recipe in *Appendix, Visual Studio Pot Pourri*

Validating your Windows Store app

Any app submitted to the Windows Store will be validated by Microsoft before being listed. Part of that validation process involves running the app through an automatic certification tool that Microsoft has included with Visual Studio 2012. You should check that your app passes the certification tool before beginning the Windows Store submission process.

Getting ready

Ensure the `SplitApp` you were using in the *Packaging your Windows Store app* recipe is working correctly and has been deployed.

For the certification process to work your deployed version must be in the **Release** mode.

How to do it...

1. From the Start screen launch the **Windows App Cert Kit**. The app will prompt for elevation and then start a wizard as shown in the following screenshot:

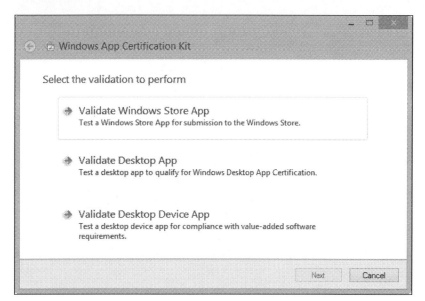

2. Select the **Validate Windows Store App** option. The tool will search for Windows Store apps installed on your machine and list them.

3. Packages are listed by the Package Display Name from the app manifest file. Locate your app and select it using the checkbox.

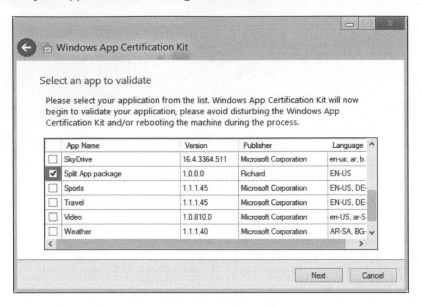

4. When the certification process completes you will be prompted to save an XML file containing the report. Choose a location to save the file to and once the file is saved you will see the completion dialog.

5. Click on the link in the dialog to view the report. The XML file you just saved will be opened in Notepad. Scan the file for warnings and errors.

How it works...

The certification kit runs your app in order to verify each of the rules it has. It does not perform tests of your app's functionality but rather validates how well the app behaves within the context of the Windows operating system and whether the rules for listing the app in the store are satisfied.

When your app passes the certification kit tests with no warnings or errors it is ready for submission to the Windows Store.

See also

▸ The *Submitting apps to the Windows Store* recipe in *Appendix, Visual Studio Pot Pourri*

3
Web Development: ASP.NET, HTML5, CSS, and JavaScript

In this chapter, we will cover:

- ▶ Creating HTML5 web pages
- ▶ Taking advantage of CSS editor improvements
- ▶ Understanding the JavaScript editor improvements
- ▶ JavaScript and CSS bundling and minification
- ▶ Verifying pages with the Page Inspector

Introduction

ASP.NET Web Development sees some significant improvements in Visual Studio 2012 and .NET Framework 4.5.

In this chapter, we will explore a number of recipes covering the changes in ASP.NET Web development for both Web Forms and MVC developers and specifically how Visual Studio 2012 supports those features.

Before we get into the recipes it is worth noting that IIS Express, released in January 2011, is now included in Visual Studio 2012 and is the default web server for ASP.NET web development. The old Visual Studio development server is still included for backward compatibility, but is no longer the default for new web projects. When you migrate your applications to Visual Studio 2012, consider switching to IIS Express if you haven't already done so.

For information on IIS Express see `http://learn.iis.net/page.aspx/860/iis-express/`.

Creating HTML5 web pages

With Visual Studio 2012, Microsoft has placed a strong focus on HTML5 and web standards in particular; partly to do with the Windows Store app development process and partly to do with being a good netizen and supporting standards based web development. This recipe will show you how Visual Studio can help you when developing a HTML5 page.

Getting ready

Simply start Visual Studio 2012 and you're ready to go.

How to do it...

1. Create a new **ASP.NET Web Forms Application** project using C# and ensure that you are targeting **.NET Framework 4.5**.

2. Open the `Site.Master` page and switch to the **Source** view in the editor.

3. In the toolbar you can change the target schema that the IDE uses to validate the markup. By default this will be based on the DOCTYPE tag in the page, though it can be manually changed. Verify that the schema is currently **DOCTYPE: HTML5**.

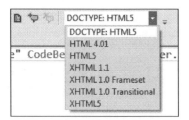

4. In the source of the page, find the `<!DOCTYPE html>` tag and edit it to match the highlighted line shown in the following screenshot:

```
<!DOCTYPE HTML PUBLIC "-//W3C//DTD HTML 4.01//EN" "http://www.w3.org/TR/html4/strict.dtd">
<html lang="en">
<head id="Head1" runat="server">
    <meta charset="utf-8" />
    <title>
```

5. Look at the validation schema in the toolbar again. It will have changed to match the document schema and will be showing as **DOCTYPE: HTML 4.01**. You should also see that the `<meta />` tag in the document is now underlined in green, indicating a validation problem:

6. What you are seeing is how Visual Studio dynamically uses DOCTYPE to validate the HTML for your page. Undo the changes to restore the DOCTYPE tag, verifying that the schema switches back to **DOCTYPE:HTML5**.

    Find the `asp:LoginView` tag in the source and click on it. You will see the standard Smart Tasks helper indicator appear.

7. Assume you need to set the users and permissions on the website. Hover over the Smart Tasks indicator until it expands to show an arrow. Click on the arrow to see the available tasks. Alternately you can press *Ctrl+.* (Ctrl+Period) to achieve the same result. From the pop-up task menu select the **Administer Website** option to open the standard ASP.NET Web Site administration page in a browser. Make any changes to the permissions you want to and then close the browser.

Feel free to explore the contents of the Smart Tasks helper and remember that it changes based on context. For example, the tasks available for the `asp:LoginView` tag will differ from that of the `asp:ScriptManager` tag.

8. Look a little further down the `Site.Master` page until you find the `<nav>` element for the menu as shown in the following screenshot:

```
<nav>
    <ul id="menu">
        <li><a href="~/" runat="server">Home</a></li>
        <li><a href="~/About.aspx" runat="server">About</a></li>
        <li><a href="~/Contact.aspx" runat="server">Contact</a></li>
    </ul>
</nav>
```

9. The `<nav>` element is a HTML5 element that wraps a group of links intended for navigation. The `nav` element in `Site.Master` can be further enhanced by adding HTML5 accessibility attributes. Select the `<nav>` element and add a space after the tag name. Visual Studio IntelliSense will automatically show a list of applicable attributes that can be added to the tag:

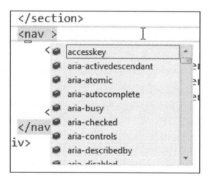

10. Enter the text **role**. IntelliSense will show the available list of roles. Select the **menu** role from the list as shown in the following screenshot:

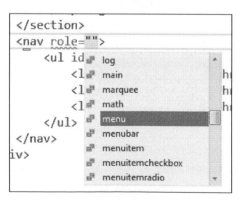

11. For accessibility reasons, list items should indicate their role as well. Select the first `<li>` element and set the role to **menuitem** and repeat this for each of the other list items in the menu.

12. Visual Studio 2012 now features code snippets in the HTML editor to help you write code faster. Let's say you want to add some elevator-style background music to your website. To do this, move the cursor below the `<nav>` element you were just working on and start to add a new `<audio>` tag by typing `<au` as shown in the following screenshot. IntelliSense will prompt you with an available code snippet you can use.

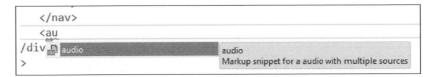

13. Press *Tab* twice to insert the snippet. Because HTML5 audio supports both `mp3` and `ogg` formatted files to cater for different browsers, two source tags are added.

```
<audio controls="controls">
    <source src="file.mp3" type="audio/mp3" />
    <source src="file.ogg" type="audio/ogg" />
</audio>
```

14. Change the name of the first audio file to `FurElise` and press *Enter*. The snippet uses a convention where the same name is used for both audio files so you should see the second source file name change automatically when you press *Enter*.

How it works...

IntelliSense in the HTML editor will filter what it displays based on the target schema used for validation. If you were to change the schema to HTML 4.01 as you did earlier in the recipe and then start to add an `<audio>` tag like we did in step 12, the snippet would not be listed as it's not applicable to HTML 4.01.

When you edit the tag name of an element that has an opening and closing tag, Visual Studio will automatically keep both tags synchronized to avoid common editing errors such as forgetting to change the matching tag or changing the wrong tag.

These improvements, and in particular the inclusion of the Smart Tasks in the **Source** view, mean there are very few reasons for web developers to switch to **Design** or **Split** views in the editor. For most developers this will be a cause for minor celebrations.

Taking advantage of CSS editor improvements

Just as in the HTML editor we looked at in the previous recipe, the Visual Studio 2012 mechanics gave the CSS editor a grease and oil change; and then added a sports exhaust, better suspension, and xenon headlights.

In this recipe we'll take a look at these improvements by tweaking the default CSS of a web project.

Getting ready

Simply start Visual Studio 2012 and you're ready to go.

How to do it...

1. Create a new **ASP.NET Web Forms Application** project in C#.

2. Open the `Content\Site.css` file.

3. Move your cursor to the hex color value in the `background-color` element of the `html` style and press *Ctrl+Space* to activate the **CSS Color Picker** as shown in the following screenshot:

```
html {
    background-color: #e2e2e2;
    margin: 0;
    padding: 0;
}
```

4. Click the down chevrons (the icon with downward facing arrows) to expand the picker to show the full gamut of colors from which you can choose. Note that the picker also lets you change the opacity of a color.

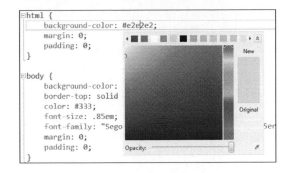

5. When building CSS for a site, sometimes you need to use a color from a picture supplied by a designer but don't have the hex value of that color. In these cases you can use the color picker to select the color value. Click on the **Color Picker** button at the bottom right of the **Color Chooser** window and then click anywhere on the screen where the color you need to use is currently showing. The color of the pixel where you click will be automatically selected for you.

6. Move the cursor down into the `body` style definition. Right-click in the selector (that is, the word `body`) and select **Build Style** from the context menu. You can also do this by opening the **Style** property editor in the **Properties** pane.

7. In the **Modify Style** dialog a **Category** list is shown with bold entries indicating categories with existing values. The dialog also includes a **Preview** of the style so you can confirm the style appears as you wish it to. Change the **Font** style so that **blink** is enabled and make **font-weight** bold. There simply aren't enough websites anymore with bold, blinking text now that Geocities no longer exists.

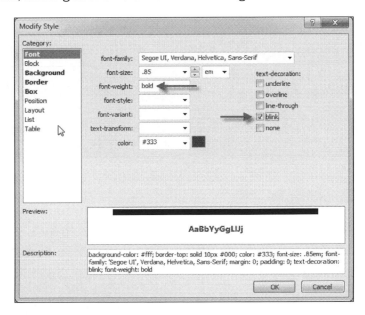

8. Click on **OK** when you have made your changes and you will be impressed with your ability to create CSS styles in a very short space of time.

9. To ensure your page is even more attention grabbing, you really should shout at your visitors. Go to the end of the `body` style and add a new blank line after the `font-weight` attribute. Type `tex` and Visual Studio will show you a list of style attributes that can be used. Select the **text-transform** attribute from the list and press *Tab*.

10. Visual Studio will now display a list of possible transforms that can be applied. Select the **uppercase** transform and press *Tab* to add it. Add a semicolon to complete the style attribute and ensure that your web page really shouts at your visitors!

```
      font-weight: bold;
      text-transform: u
}
         text-transform: Select one of the "text-transform" values
                              ⅀ᵖ  fullsize-kana
a {                           ⅀ᵖ  fullwidth
      color: #333;            ⅀ᵖ  uppercase     Puts all characters of each word in uppercase.
```

11. Locate the `ul#menu` style. You should see a number of other styles indented beneath it as shown in the following screenshot. The CSS editor has a new **hierarchical indentation** feature that can be used to indicate specificity for your styles. For example, the `ul#menu li` style is indented because it has greater specificity than the `ul#menu` style.

```
/* menu
-----------------------------------------------------------*/
ul#menu {
      font-size: 1.3em;
      font-weight: 600;
      margin: 0 0 5px;
      padding: 0;
      text-align: right;
}

      ul#menu li {
            display: inline;
            list-style: none;
            padding-left: 15px;
      }

            ul#menu li a {
                  background: none;
                  color: #999;
                  text-decoration: none;
            }

            ul#menu li a:hover {
                  color: #333;
                  text-decoration: none;
            }
```

12. You need some finishing touches to your styles. Just below the `ul#menu li a:hover` style, add a new style with a selector of `ul#menu li a:visited`.

13. Add a `color` property to the rule using any color you wish. Then press *Ctrl+K* and *Ctr+D*. This will format the document and indent it according to specificity. Your stylesheet should now look similar to the following screenshot:

```css
ul#menu li a {
    background: none;
    color: #999;
    text-decoration: none;
}

    ul#menu li a:hover {
        color: #333;
        text-decoration: none;
    }

    ul#menu li a:visited {
        color: red;
    }
```

14. The CSS editor also features code snippets, including snippets for common CSS properties that have vendor specific extensions. In the style you just added, insert a new line and type `op`. IntelliSense will show properties with "op" in their name, including an entry for the **opacity** code snippet.

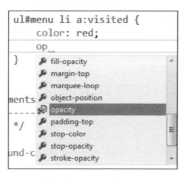

15. Select the snippet and press *Tab* twice to expand the snippet, and leave the opacity values at the defaults of `50` and `0.5`.

```css
ul#menu li a:visited {
    color: red;
    filter: alpha(opacity=50);
    -moz-opacity: 0.5;
    opacity: 0.5;
}
```

16. CSS files often have a large number of rules in them, grouped into areas, the rules for the menu being a good example. You might not want to see them all the time. The CSS editor now supports regions so you can logically group your style rules and hide them when you don't need to see them.

Head up to the existing /* menu comment. Delete both the comment and the line of dashes below it. Add a new line, /* #region menu */, in its place.

Then move to the end of the menu-related styles and add a new line, /* #endregion */. As soon as you close the comment, Visual Studio will show a document outlining indicator.

```
/* #region menu */
ul#menu {
    font-size: 1.3em;
    font-weight: 600;
                         -moz-opacity: 0.5;
                         opacity: 0.5;
                    }
/* #endregion */
```

17. Collapse the region by clicking the minus icon next to the opening #region comment.

```
menu
```

How it works...

IntelliSense in Visual Studio 2012 not only understands CSS 3.0 but also understands common browser hacks such as the star (*) and underscore (_) hacks used to target various IE specific styles. IntelliSense for style properties will still work if you start typing with a star or underscore.

When using CSS 3.0, the editor supports vendor specific extension attributes such as the -moz- and -webkit- attributes for targeting specific browsers. You saw this behavior when you used the opacity snippet in the recipe.

If you don't like the **Hierarchical Indentation** setting you can turn it off in the Visual Studio options. Go to **Tools | Options | Text Editor | CSS | Formatting** and deselect the **Hierarchical Indentation** checkbox.

The CSS editor can also be configured so that IntelliSense and validation work in CSS 3.0, CSS 2.1, or CSS 1.0 modes. Go to **Tools | Options | Text Editor | CSS | Validation** and change the drop down to the appropriate CSS level you wish to use.

 In case you are wondering, putting bold, blinking, all uppercase text on your pages is considered bad web design. It was used in this recipe as an amusing way to show you how the tools work, not as an example of how to create great styles. Unless you've got a specific reason to do this (perhaps you run a discount retail website) please don't. Your visitors will thank you!

Understanding the JavaScript editor improvements

As you have seen in the two previous recipes, the HTML and CSS editors have been greatly improved in Visual Studio 2012 and you'll be pleased to know that the JavaScript editor has also received a significant overhaul. With HTML and JavaScript being first-class choices for developing Windows Store apps it's not really a surprise that it happened.

Within the HTML5 specification the marquee tag is no longer valid, but thanks to Aaron Powell (http://www.aaron-powell.com/doing-it-wrong/marquee) we have a way to implement a marquee tag using JavaScript and jQuery. In this recipe we will write a JavaScript script to emulate a marquee tag so that we can learn how the editor works.

Getting ready

Simply start Visual Studio 2012 and you're ready to go.

How to do it...

1. Create a new **ASP.NET Web Forms Application** project.

2. Add a new JavaScript file named `marquee.js` to the `Scripts` folder in your solution.

3. The original marquee tag scrolled a block element horizontally across the page. For this to work in JavaScript you first need to know the width of the element you will be animating.

   In your empty `marquee.js` file start by typing the jQuery shortcut `$` character followed by a period (`.`) to bring up the IntelliSense options.

IntelliSense should now be showing you all the valid jQuery functions you can use along with their method signatures.

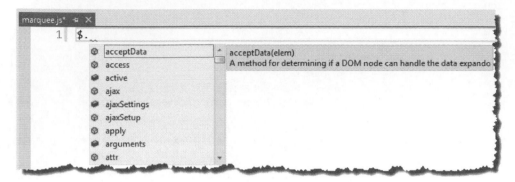

4. Enter the following JavaScript script in `marquee.js`:

```javascript
$.fn.textwidth = function () {
    var calc = '<span style="display:none">'
        + $(this).text() + '</span>';
    $('body').append(calc);
    var width = $('body').find('span:last').width();
    $('body').find('span:last').remove();
    return width;
};
```

5. At this point you have a simple method for returning the width of the text. You can now start writing the marquee function by adding the following JavaScript script at the bottom of the `marquee.js` file:

```javascript
$.fn.marquee = function () {
    var that = $(this),
        calculatedWidth = that.textwidth(),
        offset = calculatedWidth,
        width = offset;
};
```

6. Before you go any further, put your cursor on the `textwidth()` method call in the line you just added and either press *F12* or right-click it and select **Go To Definition**.

7. Visual Studio will navigate to where the `textwidth()` method definition is declared. In the `textwidth()` method, move the cursor onto the call to the jQuery `append()` method and press *F12* to go to its definition. You will be taken to the method in the `jquery-1.6.2-vsdoc.js` file.

If you update your jQuery version, either manually or via NuGet, then you will be taken to a different version of the `-vsdoc.js` file than the one shown in the recipe.

8. It's time to finish off the JavaScript you were working on before. Navigate back to the `marquee.js` file by pressing *Ctrl+-* (*Ctrl* and the minus key) to navigate backwards. Complete the first part of the marquee function by ensuring the CSS used in the animation is defined. Replace the existing `width = offset;` statement with the following code (note the change of the semicolon to a comma on the first line):

```
$.fn.marquee = function () {
    var that = $(this),
    calculatedWidth = that.textwidth(),
    offset - calculatedWidth,
    width = offset,  ◄━━━
    css = {
        'text-indent': that.css('text-indent'),
        'overflow': that.css('overflow'),
        'white-space': that.css('white-space')
    },
    marqueeCss = {
        'text-indent': width,
        'overflow': 'hidden',
        'white-space': 'nowrap'
    };
};
```

9. Complete the method by adding the following highlighted code to the marquee function. The `go()` function is used as the main loop of the marquee effect and adjusts the CSS of the element each time through the loop, before using the `setTimeout` method to pause execution before looping again.

```
    marqueeCss = {
        'text-indent': width,
        'overflow': 'hidden',
        'white-space': 'nowrap'
    };
    function go() {
        if (width == (calculatedWidth * -1)) {
            width = offset;
        }
        that.css('text-indent', width + 'px');
        width--;
        setTimeout(go, 1e1);
    };
    that.css(marqueeCss);
    width--;
    go();
};
```

10. You may have noticed that, as you typed the inner `go()` function in the editor, the outlining tips appeared. This is a new feature in Visual Studio 2012 to help with document outlining. The collapsed `go()` method is shown in the following screenshot:

```
};
function go()[...];
that.css(marqueeCss);
```

11. Now all that's left is to apply the marquee function to a web page! In **Solution Explorer** navigate to the `About.aspx` page and view the HTML source.

    Move to the bottom of the HTML file and just before the closing `</asp:Content>` tag, add a reference to the marquee script.

```
    </aside>
    <script src="/Scripts/marquee.js"></script>
</asp:Content>
```

12. The `<p>` element would make a good target for your marquee script. Add another script block directly below the reference you added in the previous step and enter `$('p').marquee();` in the body of the script.

    As you type, IntelliSense will provide information on the available methods, including your newly-created marquee method, as shown in the following screenshot:

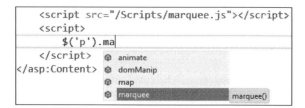

13. Run the application and navigate to the `About.aspx` page to see the marquee in action. Simply awesome! Maybe that's overstating it a little, but it was certainly fun!

How it works...

When you first started typing the marquee script and IntelliSense displayed the jQuery information, you may have been wondering where that information came from. IntelliSense uses the contents of the `_references.js` file to discover information about the JavaScript libraries for your project.

If you don't like this file or have another convention you wish to use then you can customize this behavior through the Visual Studio options under **Text Editor | JavaScript | IntelliSense | References**, selecting the **Implicit (Web)** group.

There's more...

Visual Studio supports ECMAScript 5 and IntelliSense will show ECMAScript methods whenever appropriate. For example, the `trim()` method will be displayed for string variables but not for numeric variables.

If you want good page load times with JavaScript you should be placing your scripts at the bottom of your page, with the exception of modernizr. In the `About.aspx` page you placed the scripts at the bottom of the page but, since that page is actually loaded into an ASP.NET content control on a master page, the scripts would be rendered mid-page. Not quite what you want.

 For more information on the impact of JavaScript positioning and the impact on page load times see the Yahoo! Best Practices for Speeding up Your Web Site list at `http://developer.yahoo.com/performance/rules.html`.

A better approach might be to add a new content placeholder to the master page called, for example, **EndOfPageScripts,** and place it below the `<footer />` element. In the `About.aspx` file you could then add a second ASP.NET content control for the **EndOfPageScripts** placeholder and place the scripts there.

Regions

The JavaScript editor does not support regions. Personally I'm very glad about that since developers often use them to hide ugly and problematic code rather than fixing it. They do however have a legitimate use at times. So if you desperately want to add region support to Visual Studio 2012 keep an eye on the Visual Studio gallery. For example, region support in Visual Studio 2010 is available via the JSEnhancements extension at `http://visualstudiogallery.msdn.microsoft.com/0696ad60-1c68-4b2a-9646-4b5f4f8f2e06/` and at the time of writing, there is a preliminary version available for Visual Studio 2012 available in the gallery and also at `https://jsoutlining11.codeplex.com/`.

JavaScript and CSS bundling and minification

One of the common techniques for improving website performance is to reduce the number of requests a browser needs to make in order to get the resources required for the page, and to compress any resources that are requested to reduce bandwidth.

When it comes to both JavaScript and CSS, this generally means combining all of the files of the same type into a single large file (**bundling**) and then removing unnecessary whitespace from them and renaming variables to use the minimum amount of space possible, while still leaving the functionality unchanged (**minification**).

ASP.NET 4.5 supports automatic bundling and minification and in this recipe you'll add bundling and minification to a site and see how it impacts your development activities.

Getting ready

We're going to use the project from the previous recipe, *Understanding the JavaScript editor improvements*. If you haven't already done so, complete that recipe.

If you don't have time, the completed code from the previous recipe is located in the `Chapter 3\Marquee.zip` archive for you to use as your starting point.

The recipe assumes that your browser of choice has developer tools that are able to capture network traffic. If you use Internet Explorer you will need Internet Explorer 9 or later, which is what this recipe will assume you are using.

How to do it...

1. Build the application and run it without the debugger by pressing *Ctrl+F5* or choosing **Debug | Start Without Debugging** from the menu.

2. Navigate to the `http://<yoursite>/About.aspx` page in your browser and open the browser's developer tools. If you are using Internet Explorer 9 then you can press *F12* to open them.

3. Go to the **Network** tab and click on the **Start Capturing** button. Press *Ctrl+F5* to force a full refresh of the page. The network trace should show that a lot of files are required to load the page as shown in the following screenshot:

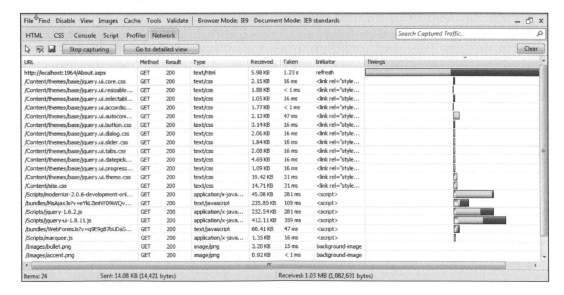

4. Look at all those requests! If you want a faster loading page, you need to reduce this. Leaving the browser open, switch back to Visual Studio and in **Solution Explorer** find and open the `Site.Master` file.

5. In that file, at line 13, you will find the code shown in the following screenshot:

```
<asp:PlaceHolder runat="server">
    <%: Styles.Render("~/Content/themes/base/css", "~/Content/css") %>
    <%: Scripts.Render("~/bundles/modernizr") %>
</asp:PlaceHolder>
```

6. The `Scripts.Render()` statement is outputting a `~/bundles/modernizr` file. Look at **Solution Explorer** again. There is no `bundles` folder. What's going on here?

7. In **Solution Explorer** expand the `App_Start` folder and then open the `BundleConfig` file within that. The third statement of the `RegisterBundles()` method defines the missing file.

```
bundles.Add(new ScriptBundle("~/bundles/modernizr").Include(
    "~/Scripts/modernizr-*"));
```

8. In your projects you will no doubt want bundles for your own custom JavaScript, so create one now by adding a new statement to the `RegisterBundles()` method as follows:

```
bundles.Add(new ScriptBundle("~/bundles/customjs").Include(
    "~/Scripts/marquee.js"));
```

9. Go back to `Site.Master` and at the bottom of the page include a reference to your `customjs` bundle, as shown in the following screenshot:

```
    </form>
    <%: Scripts.Render("~/bundles/customjs") %>
</body>
```

10. Go to the `About.aspx` page and remove the script reference for the `marquee.js` file. Since the marquee function won't be present when it's called in the `About.aspx` page, change the call to only happen when the page is ready, as follows:

```
<script>
    $(function () { $('p').marquee(); });
</script>
```

11. Rebuild the solution, switch over to your browser and perform a full page refresh (that is, *Ctrl+F5* in Internet Explorer). Assuming the network tab is still open in the developer tools, you should see the `marquee.js` file being loaded and the marquee effect still working.

12. While you have defined the bundles, they still aren't actually being bundled or minified. Switch back to Visual Studio and in **Solution Explorer** find and open `Global.asax.cs`. In the `Application_Start()` method add the following highlighted line of code to enable optimizations:

```
void Application_Start(object sender, EventArgs e)
{
    // Code that runs on application startup
    BundleConfig.RegisterBundles(BundleTable.Bundles);
    BundleTable.EnableOptimizations = true;
}
```

The `EnableOptimizations` call forces bundling to occur. Without this call bundling only occurs when running the site in release mode. In other words, when the `debug="true"` attribute of the `system.web.compilation` tag of the `web.config` file is specified, bundling optimizations are disabled.

13. Rebuild the application, switch over to the browser and perform a full page refresh again. The network trace will now show that JavaScript bundles are being downloaded instead of individual script files and that the download size of the bundle files is less than the download size of the original JavaScript files, as shown in the following screenshot:

URL	Method	Result	Type	Received	Taken
http://localhost:1964/About.aspx	GET	200	text/html	5.22 KB	6.34 s
/Content/themes/base/css?v=UM624qf1u...	GET	200	text/css	24.86 KB	1.48 s
/Content/css?v=1KFY-7bppjbhzN_j-uZ7aD...	GET	200	text/css	8.42 KB	1.48 s
/bundles/modernizr?v=EuTZa4MRY0ZqCY...	GET	200	text/javascript	10.30 KB	1.77 s
/bundles/MsAjaxJs?v=eYkLZimNY09iWQv...	GET	200	text/javascript	235.85 KB	2.23 s
/Scripts/jquery-1.6.2.js	GET	200	application/x-java...	232.54 KB	1.57 s
/Scripts/jquery-ui-1.8.11.js	GET	200	application/x-java...	412.11 KB	1.73 s
/bundles/WebFormsJs?v=a9E9a87bUDaS...	GET	200	text/javascript	60.41 KB	1.82 s
/bundles/customjs?v=YRnrMMmFsRGsYGR...	GET	200	text/javascript	0.94 KB	1.76 s
/Images/bullet.png	GET	200	image/png	3.20 KB	15 ms
/Images/accent.png	GET	200	image/png	0.92 KB	< 1 ms
/Images/twitter.png	GET	200	image/png	0.88 KB	< 1 ms
/Images/facebook.png	GET	200	image/png	0.92 KB	15 ms

14. It's worth confirming that the scripts are not only bundled but also minified. Navigate to the **Script** tab in the browser developer tools and select the `customjs` file from the scripts drop-down list:

15. Use the search box on the right to locate the **marquee** function as shown in the following screenshot. In the script you can see that, not only has the whitespace been removed, but the variable names have also been shortened and the code slightly optimized. Exactly what you should expect minification to do.

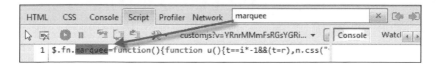

How it works...

Inside the ASP.NET runtime, when a browser requests a page with a bundle in it, ASP.NET will either render the names of the individual files in the bundle or the bundle name itself, depending on whether optimizations are turned on or not. When optimizations are on, browsers will request bundles by their name and ASP.NET will group the individual bundled files into a single larger file before minifying them and sending the result back to the browser. The resulting minified file is cached by ASP.NET so that future requests do not impact site performance.

You can create your own custom bundle types by subclassing the `Bundle` class allowing you to do pretty much anything you need to provide your own minification rules and bundling mechanisms, which may be useful if you want to support web technologies such as LESS, Sass, or CoffeeScript, for example.

See also

  ▶ The *Understanding the JavaScript editor improvements* recipe

Verifying pages with the Page Inspector

The **Page Inspector** is a tool provided with Visual Studio that comprises a browser that runs inside Visual Studio and a range of page inspection tools similar to what is provided with the Internet Explorer developer tools, but with the ability to map elements back to the line of code that generated them.

The page inspector is so good that you can almost hear a TV shopping channel's shouty man doing an advert like this: "See something that doesn't look right on your web pages? You're not sure where it came from? You're wondering how on earth you'll track it down? Well, fear not, for the Page Inspector is here! All new Page Inspector will do the dirty detective work for you and pinpoint the sneaky culprit! For a single up-front payment and 12 easy installments you too can own the Page Inspector! Order now and you'll also get these free steak knives and a squeaky penguin toy for your kids! Call now!!"

Well, maybe not.:-)

Let's put that silliness aside and have a look at what the Page Inspector can really do for your debugging experience by following this recipe.

Getting ready

The Page Inspector requires Internet Explorer 9 (or later).

If you are developing on a Windows Server operating system you must have Internet Explorer Enhanced Security Configuration disabled.

How to do it...

1. Create a new C# **ASP.NET MVC 4 Internet Application** project using the **Razor** view engine and give it the default name.

2. You can launch the Page Inspector from the **View | Other Windows | Page Inspector** menu, the **Quick Launch** tool, by right-clicking a page and selecting **View In Page Inspector,** by clicking the Page Inspector icon in the toolbar, or by pressing *Ctrl+K and Ctrl+G.*

   For this recipe, right-click on the `Views\Home\Index.cshtml` page and select **View in Page Inspector**.

3. The Page Inspector will open in a tool window next to the main document area and display the site's home page.

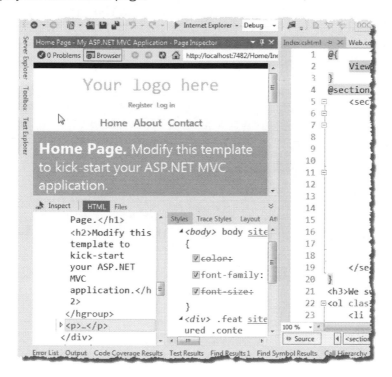

4. In the bottom half of the Page Inspector is a toolbar with a number of inspection tabs and also an **Inspect** button. Click that and then click on the **Your logo here** text of the web page in the top section of the inspector. As you do, you will notice that the HTML tab adjusts to show the relevant part of the DOM, and that the code where the text came from is shown in the document pane.

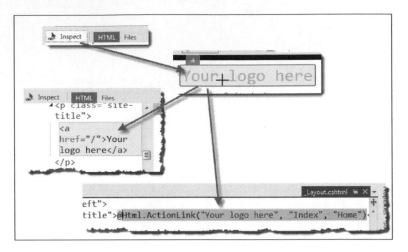

5. Inside the `Views\Shared\_Layout.cshtml` file, which should currently be open in the document area, move to the bottom of the file and locate the footer element. Highlight a section of the copyright notice, as shown, and note how the matching text in the Page Inspector is highlighted. You will also see that the HTML tab of the Page Inspector updates to show the page DOM and that the other Page Inspector tabs update to reflect the details of the selected item. This bi-directional selection is very nice and very, very useful.

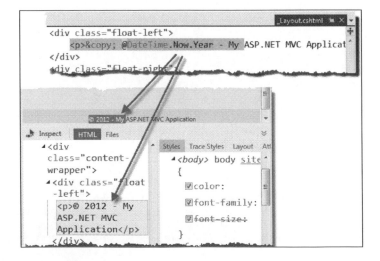

6. With the text still highlighted, select the **Trace Styles** tab in the Page Inspector and scroll down to the `margin-top` attribute. Expand the item and click on the `footer p` selector. When you do so, the `site.css` file will be shown and the `footer p` style highlighted. This gives you a great way to trace a style you see on a page directly back to the source file it came from.

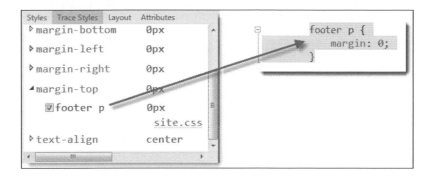

 If you can't find the style, you may have accidentally changed the selected content in the Page Inspector. Try reselecting the copyright notice and then looking at the **Trace Styles** tab again.

7. Change the `margin` properties of the style in the `Site.css` file to `margin: 10px 0 0 0;`.

8. The **Page Inspector** detects that a change has occurred and displays an informational message prompting you to save your changes and refresh the page. Do so by clicking the message or pressing *Ctrl+Alt+Enter* to see the change to the footer.

How it works...

When you first launched the Page Inspector you didn't need to compile the web application or launch IIS Express. The Page Inspector did that for you automatically, making the process of getting started very simple.

The mapping of the page elements and styles back to the source only works if those elements are statically generated. In other words, they have to map back to the actual source and can't be the result of any dynamic DOM manipulation performed via JavaScript. The mapping of page elements to the JavaScript that created them is not supported by the Page Inspector.

There's more...

One thing you didn't look at in the recipe was the **Files** tab, located next to the **HTML** tab in the Page Inspector. The **Files** tab shows all the source files that were used in the construction of the layout for the page, excluding CSS and JavaScript files.

Partial pages and user controls

If you right-click a partial view or a user control in **Solution Explorer** and select **View in Page Inspector**, the Page Inspector may not be able to determine how to launch those pages because the routing rules aren't specific enough or for some other reason. When this happens the Page Inspector will prompt you for a URL to navigate to that includes the view or control you are interested in:

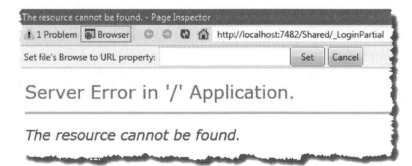

Enter an absolute or relative URL and then click on **Set** to define the mapping. The next time you inspect the user control or partial page, the Page Inspector will remember your mapping and launch the appropriate page for you, allowing you to inspect your element in the context of the containing page.

The Page Inspector is too narrow!

By default the Page Inspector is loaded in a tool window on the left of the IDE and renders the page in a very narrow window.

You don't have to live with it this way. If you have multiple monitors then you can undock the Page Inspector and drag it over to your second monitor. You will then be able to see the full page in the Page Inspector as well as your code, and the two-way synchronization of code and HTML will be easy to track.

Alternatively you can move the Page Inspector to the main document area, though doing so will mean that you have to use *Ctrl+Tab* to switch between the Page Inspector and the source files.

Of course, the final option is to simply widen the Page Inspector tool window, though doing so reduces the size of the main document area. Regardless, if the window is too narrow for your liking, change it! It's your Visual Studio; make it work the way you want it to.

4

.NET Framework 4.5 Development

In this chapter, we will cover:

- ► Adding the Ribbon to a WPF application
- ► Creating a state machine in Visual Studio 2012
- ► Creating a Task-based WCF service
- ► Managing packages with NuGet
- ► Unit testing .NET applications
- ► Sharing class libraries across runtimes
- ► Detecting duplicate code

Introduction

In Chapter 3, Web Development: ASP.NET, HTML5, CSS, and JavaScript, we looked at web development and how Visual Studio supports web developers. In this chapter we turn the spotlight on Visual Studio 2012's support for developers using the other major .NET technologies and how it promotes good development practices in general. We will look specifically at functionality that has been added or enhanced.

First, you should be aware that the .NET Framework 4.5 is an in-place upgrade of .NET Framework 4.0. It is backward compatible with all .NET Framework 4.0 functionality and encompasses both of the runtime profiles that .NET 4.0 provided.

On those profiles, the approach of having two .NET 4.0 redistributables (client and full) has ended with .NET 4.5. It is now a single runtime only. When building .NET 4.5, Microsoft realized that the size difference between the two profiles was insignificant and any potential deployment savings couldn't be justified compared to the cost of testing applications against two versions of the runtime, plus the single redistributable simplifies the overall deployment story. Of course, there is a new profile for Windows 8 with the Windows Store profile for .NET Framework 4.5, however it comes preinstalled with Window 8 and there is no downloadable redistributable.

> Be aware that .NET Framework 4.5 is not supported on Windows XP, Windows Vista, or Windows Server 2003.
>
> Extended support for Windows XP SP3 ends in 2014. Extended support for Windows Server 2003 ends in 2015 and the user base for Windows Vista is small. For this reason the lack of framework support for those operating systems shouldn't be a problem.

Adding the Ribbon to a WPF application

Windows Presentation Foundation (**WPF**) is still the preferred platform for developing desktop applications on the Windows platform. Visual Studio 2012 itself is a WPF application and, even with Windows 8, there will still be many applications that are going to target the Windows Desktop.

For developers of desktop applications it is good to know that WPF continues to receive updates and enhancements. In .NET 4.5 you can now use the provided Ribbon control in your applications and in this recipe you will see how this is done.

Getting ready

You'll need some icons for this recipe. The ones you'll be using for this recipe can be downloaded from `http://www.windowsico.com/download.htm` and are licensed under the Creative Commons license. The specific download you are looking for is the **VistaICO Aero Pack**. Credit goes to `VistaIco.com` for making these icons available. Make sure you have downloaded these icons before starting this recipe; alternatively have a set of your own you can use instead.

Start Visual Studio 2012 and create a new C# WPF Application using the default name.

How to do it...

1. You need to add a reference to the Ribbon control in order to use it. Right-click the project in **Solution Explorer** and add a reference to the `System.Windows.Controls.Ribbon` assembly.

2. The easiest way to work with the Ribbon is to edit the XAML directly as there are a number of child controls that need to be added. Open the `MainWindow.xaml` file and change the markup so that the base class is no longer a `<Window>` control but a `<RibbonWindow>` control.

3. You need to make a similar change in the code behind file. Navigate to the `MainWindows.xaml.cs` file and change the base class from `Window` to `RibbonWindow` and add a `using` statement for `System.Window.Controls. Ribbon` to the file as well.

   Switch back to the designer. Add a Ribbon control to the form by adding a `<Ribbon>` element inside the `<Grid>` element as shown. As you do so the Ribbon will appear in the designer window.

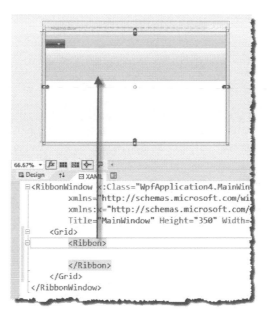

4. The Ribbon hosts tabs, groups, and buttons (amongst other things), so populate the Ribbon by adding the following XAML code:

```xml
<Ribbon>
    <RibbonTab x:Name="FirstTab" Header="Tab1">
        <RibbonGroup Header="Group 1">
            <RibbonButton Background="Azure" Label="Button 1" />
            <RibbonButton Background="AliceBlue" Label="Button 2" />
        </RibbonGroup>
        <RibbonGroup Header="Group 2">
            <RibbonButton Background="Bisque" Label="Button 3" />
            <RibbonButton Background="MintCream" Label="Button 4" />
        </RibbonGroup>
    </RibbonTab>
    <RibbonTab Header="Tab2">
        <RibbonGroup Header="Group 3">
            <RibbonButton Background="Purple" Label="Button 5" />
            <RibbonButton Background="Pink" Label="Button 6" />
        </RibbonGroup>
    </RibbonTab>
</Ribbon>
```

5. Run the application to check that the Ribbon control appears correctly and that you can switch between tab groups. The application should look like the following screenshot. Close the application when you have confirmed things are working.

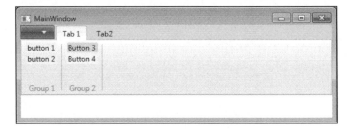

6. The Ribbon control also features a **Quick Access Toolbar** and an **Application Menu**. Add a Quick Access Toolbar by adding the following code between `<Ribbon>` and `<RibbonTab>` as shown in the following screenshot:

```xml
<Ribbon>
    <Ribbon.QuickAccessToolBar>
        <RibbonQuickAccessToolBar>
            <RibbonQuickAccessToolBar.Items>
                <RibbonButton Background="Red" />
                <RibbonButton Background="Orange" />
            </RibbonQuickAccessToolBar.Items>
        </RibbonQuickAccessToolBar>
    </Ribbon.QuickAccessToolBar>
    <RibbonTab x:Name="FirstTab" Header="Tab1">
```

7. Run the application again to confirm that the Quick Access Toolbar is appearing correctly:

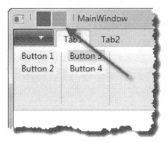

8. At this point it's time to add some images to those buttons. Start by adding an Images folder to your project.

9. From Windows Explorer, unzip the Vista Icons pack (you should have downloaded this before starting the recipe) into the Images folder.

10. In Visual Studio, click on the **Show All Files** icon in **Solution Explorer**. Select all the files in the Images folder, right-click them, and select **Include in Project**.

11. Hover the mouse over one of the image files in the Images folder. You will see a preview of what each image looks like. Such a handy little feature!

12. Edit the `MainWindow.xaml` file to replace each button background with an image. The `QuickAccessToolbar` uses the `SmallImageSource` attribute for images and the main `RibbonTab` buttons use the `LargeImageSource` attribute.

Make the changes for as many buttons as you like using the images you prefer.

You can avoid typing full path names by entering just the attribute name and then dragging the image to use onto the XAML editor from **Solution Explorer** as shown. Just remember to change the image path so that it is a relative path, not an absolute one.

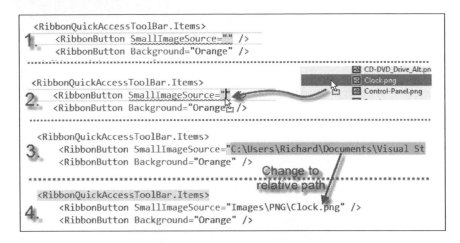

13. Run the program to confirm that the Ribbon control is looking the way you want it to.

How it works...

While this recipe shows you how to lay out the new WPF Ribbon, it is hardly an exhaustive run through of the Ribbon control and nor is it meant to be. The recipe is to show you how Visual Studio assists you when developing WPF applications.

You should have also noticed that the WPF designer feels better to use and more responsive than the Visual Studio 2010 designer and that it keeps up with your XAML changes better than before. This will make developing WPF and XAML applications in general a lot smoother than previously and it should remove some of the angst people have had with Visual Studio's XAML designer.

Beyond the Ribbon, WPF also includes features such as asynchronous validation and the ability to access collections on non-UI threads without needing to marshal calls. These extra features, along with the improved binding, async language features, and general .NET 4.5 runtime enhancements should help you to deliver Windows Desktop applications that feel more responsive for your users and don't suffer from the white screen of death anywhere near as often.

See also

▸ The *Making your code asynchronous* recipe in *Chapter 6, Asynchrony in .NET*

Creating a state machine in Visual Studio 2012

Windows Workflow underwent a major overhaul for .NET 4.0 and was largely a ground up rewrite. As part of that rewrite the workflow designer was also rebuilt; however it was fairly slow and in medium to large workflows was more than capable of crashing Visual Studio, taking all your unsaved changes with it and generally annoying anyone who had to use it for long periods of time.

In Visual Studio 2012 the workflow designer has been given some tender loving care and encouraged to behave more like a grown up.

For the workflow engine itself, Microsoft has added much needed support for state machines. Let's have a look at how to put one together.

Getting ready

Start Visual Studio 2012 and create a new **Visual Basic | Workflow | Activity Library** project.

How to do it...

1. The `Activity1.xaml` file should be open in the designer when the project is created, but if it isn't, open it now.

2. In the **Toolbox** you will see the workflow activities from Visual Studio 2010 as well as a new group called **State Machine**. From within that group drag a **StateMachine** activity onto the `Activity1.xaml` designer.

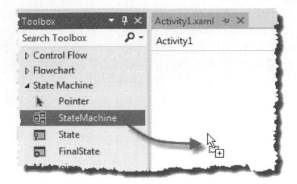

3. Drag a **State** activity onto the state machine you just added in the designer. You should now have two states as shown in the following screenshot:

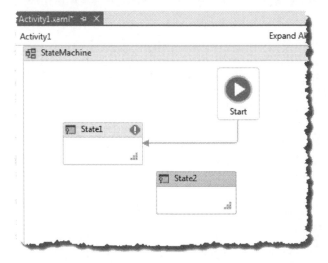

4. Next, position your mouse near the edge of **State1** as shown in the following screenshot. A connector drag handle will appear (1). Click-and-drag it to join **State1** to **State2** (2). When you let go of the mouse the transition will be given a default name of **T1** (3).

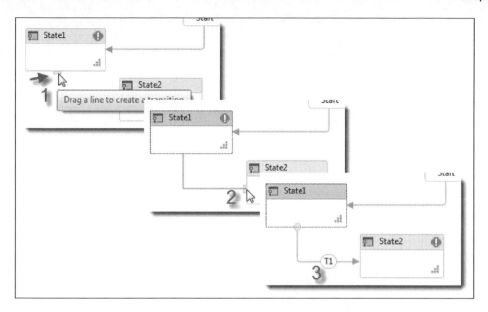

5. All state machine workflows need a final state, so drag a **FinalState** activity onto the state machine and add transitions from the existing states to the final state as shown in the following screenshot:

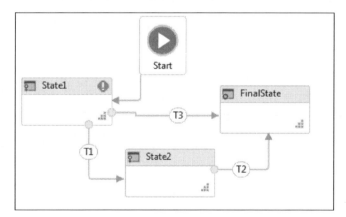

6. The default naming of states doesn't make much sense from a readability perspective. Click in the headers of each state to edit their names and name them **New Task**, **In Progress**, and **Closed** as shown in the following screenshot:

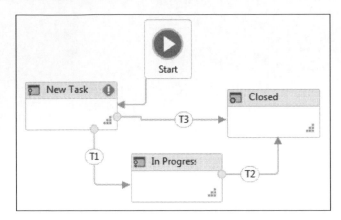

7. To rename the state transitions you will need to double-click each one and then click the header to edit the description. Change the transition names to **Commenced**, **Cancelled**, and **Completed** as shown in the following screenshot:

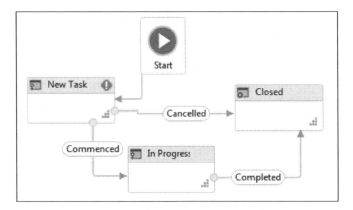

8. At the top right of the **New Task** state is a blue warning symbol. This exists because there are two possible transitions from **New Task** to other states.

    The workflow engine needs a way to choose between the two transitions. Add an argument to your workflow by clicking the **Arguments** tab at the bottom of the designer.

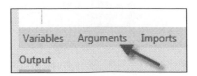

9. Click on the **Create Argument** line to create a new entry. Leave the argument name as the default one but change the **Argument type** to **Boolean** as shown in the following screenshot:

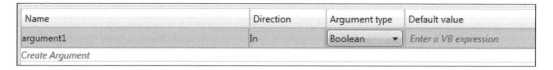

Name	Direction	Argument type	Default value
argument1	In	Boolean ▾	*Enter a VB expression*
Create Argument			

10. Double-click the **Commenced** transition in the designer, and in the **Condition** enter `argument1 = True` as shown in the following screenshot:

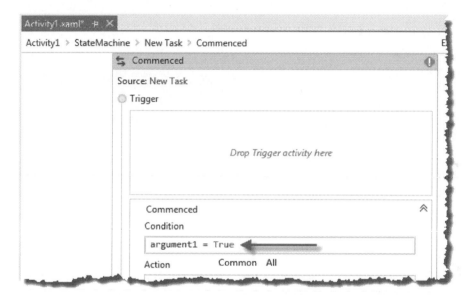

 Because `argument1` is a Boolean the `= True` comparison is redundant. It is used here to aid readability and maintainability.

11. Return to the state machine view in the designer by clicking on **StateMachine** in the breadcrumbs, located at the top of the designer.

12. Set the condition on the **Cancelled** transition to `Not argument1` using the same method you used in step 10.

13. Return again to the state machine view and note how the **New Tasks** state no longer shows you the warning icon because there is now a way to choose between the transitions. Build the application to ensure the workflow is defined correctly.

How it works...

State machines are a very welcome addition to the Windows Workflow functionality and are useful in many situations. It isn't shown in the recipe, but each state has entry and exit actions that are activated as the state machine transitions between states, and can be used to customize how the workflow behaves.

Upon entering a state the entry action is processed and when the action is complete the Trigger for each possible state transition is prepared. Triggers are effective event listeners and state transitions only occur when a trigger event has been received and the **Condition** evaluates to `true`. The Workflow runtime provides a number of trigger activities, though in many cases you will need to create your own trigger activities specifically for your purposes.

There's more...

You can now search within workflows! Hooray! If you've ever dealt with large workflows then you'll be well aware of the pain of not having a search feature.

Quick Find (Visual Studio's normal find function) will match on object properties, variables, arguments, and expressions.

Find in Files will search the XAML representation of the workflow and match on anything it finds in there. When double-clicking a search result, the designer will navigate to the activity that matches the search result location.

Panning

Such a simple thing to improve usability and it's finally here!

Pan the designer either by dragging with the middle mouse button, or by holding down space and dragging with the left mouse button.

Alternately, click on the panning icon at the bottom-right of the designer.

C# Workflows

In previous versions of Visual Studio all workflow projects required expressions to be entered using the Visual Basic syntax. With Visual Studio 2012 C# workflow, projects will now use C# expressions.

If you upgrade an existing workflow from .NET 4.0 to .NET 4.5, a compatibility flag is set on the workflow so that any existing Visual Basic expressions will still work.

Versioning your workflows

Versioning problems have long hindered the adoption of Windows Workflow. Changing a workflow definition could easily break long running, persisted workflows and cause applications to crash or data to be lost.

With Visual Studio 2012 a new `WorkflowIdentity` class has been added for dealing with persisted workflows. `WorkflowIdentity` allows you to host multiple versions of a workflow side-by-side so that your old persisted workflows can still run through to completion while new workflows will use the new definitions you provide.

In addition, `DynamicUpdate` can be used to amend the definition of older, persisted workflows if you want to bring them in line with your newer workflow definitions.

Creating a Task-based WCF service

There's not a great deal of change in Visual Studio 2012 for Windows Communication Foundation (WCF) development. However, don't misread that as there's not a lot of improvement for WCF developers in .NET Framework 4.5, as that's far from the truth! It's simply that since WCF is a technology focused on network communications, the changes in Visual Studio 2012 are quite small.

The only visible changes are in the **Add Service Reference** dialog and the IntelliSense support for WCF configurations.

In this recipe you'll create a Task-based WCF service so that you can see what has changed.

Getting ready

Simply start Visual Studio 2012 and you're ready to go.

How to do it...

1. Create a new project using the **Visual C# | WCF | WCF Service Application** template and give it the default name.

2. Add to the solution another project using the **Visual C# | Windows | WPF Application** template, also giving it the default name.

3. Compile the solution and start the WCF service to make sure it starts correctly and so that you have a working service for the next few steps. Stop the application once you are happy that it's working.

4. Back in Visual Studio, right-click on the WPF application and select **Add Service Reference**.

5. Click on the **Discover** button. The **Service1** web service should be discovered.

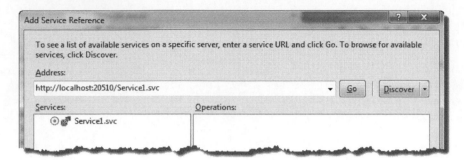

6. Click on the **Advanced** button in the bottom-left of the **Add Service Reference** dialog. Ensure that, in the options for service generation, **Generate task-based operations** is selected and **Allow generation of asynchronous operations** is turned on.

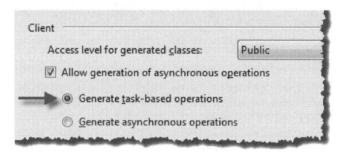

7. Click on **OK** in the options dialog and then in the **Add Service Reference** dialog to generate the service proxy.

8. Go to the `app.config` file for the WPF application, locate the `<endpoint>` configuration section, and hover the mouse over the name attribute. A tooltip will appear to explain what this attribute is for. Given the issues people have historically had with understanding the details in WCF configuration, this IntelliSense information is very welcome.

```
<endpoint address="http://localhost:20510/Service1.svc" bindi
    bindingConfiguration="BasicHttpBinding_IService1" contrac
    name="BasicHttpBinding_IService1" />
lient Optional string attribute. This attribute uniquely identifies an endpoint for a given contract.
m.serviceModel>
```

9. Start to add a new endpoint configuration to the `<client />` section by typing `<endpoint binding=`. IntelliSense will kick in to show you the values that can be placed inside the quotes. That makes editing WCF configurations much simpler than trying to remember what all the valid values are. Select the **basicHttpsBinding** value.

10. Continue building the endpoint configuration by adding a `bindingConfiguration` attribute. When you type the = (equals), IntelliSense will pop up again and show you the binding configurations available as well as a tooltip about the binding. Helpful! Select the **BasicHttpBinding_IService1** option and then close the endpoint configuration element with `/ >`.

 The endpoint you just added is not yet complete. The recipe asks you to add it so you can see the new IntelliSense support for WCF configurations. Once you finish the recipe, try manually adding support for `basicHttpsBinding` by editing the `.config` files and using the HTTPS endpoint for communications.

11. In the WPF project, open `MainWindow.xaml` and change the `<Grid>` to a `<StackPanel>`. Add a button and a textbox to the `StackPanel` as shown in the following screenshot:

```
<StackPanel>
    <Button x:Name="btnAsync" Click="btnAsync_Click_1">Click!</Button>
    <TextBlock x:Name="txtText">Not yet populated</TextBlock>
</StackPanel>
```

12. Navigate to the code behind file, `MainWindow.xaml.cs`, and add code for the button click event handler so that it calls out to the WCF service, as follows:

```
async private void btnAsync_Click_1(object sender, RoutedEventArgs e)
{
    using (var client = new ServiceReference1.Service1Client())
    {
        var result = await client.GetDataAsync(3);
        txtText.Text = result;
    }
}
```

13. In **Solution Explorer**, right-click the solution and select the **Set StartUp Projects** option.

14. Choose **Multiple startup projects** and set **Action** to **Start** for both projects. Click on **OK** to save the changes.

15. Press *F5* to start debugging and, when the WPF application appears, click on the **Click!** button to make the async call to the WCF service.

    The text below the button should update to say **You entered: 3**, proving the call to the service worked.

How it works...

As mentioned, the **Add Service Reference** dialog can generate Task-based proxy classes that you can call from your code with an `await` keyword. This makes asynchronous calls to services much easier to write, though you can still call the blocking, synchronous methods if you really want to.

The generated code contains both the synchronous method call as well as the Task-based call as shown in the following screenshot:

```
[System.CodeDom.Compiler.GeneratedCodeAttribute("System.ServiceModel", "4.0.0.0")]
[System.ServiceModel.ServiceContractAttribute(ConfigurationName="ServiceReference1.IService1")]
public interface IService1 {

    [System.ServiceModel.OperationContractAttribute(Action="http://tempuri.org/IService1/GetData",
    string GetData(int value);

    [System.ServiceModel.OperationContractAttribute(Action="http://tempuri.org/IService1/GetData",
    System.Threading.Tasks.Task<string> GetDataAsync(int value);
}
```

WCF's svcutil can also be used to generate Task-based proxies if you prefer to use the command-line tool instead of Visual Studio.

See Also

▶ The *Making your code asynchronous* recipe *Chapter 6, Asynchrony in .NET*

Managing packages with NuGet

Microsoft's approach to Open Source software and Open Source projects in general has softened over the years from the "open source is evil" stance it took at the turn of the century, to one where open source is now valued, embraced, and recognized as an integral part of the development ecosystem. Microsoft is now so committed to open source that they are developing a number of frameworks in an open manner including the ASP.NET Web Stack (`http://aspnetwebstack.codeplex.com`) and providing contributions for a number of third-party open source projects such as jQuery and Node.js.

With the amount of open source now available and the acceptance of open source as a normal part of development, developers needed an easy way to locate and find open source packages that could be used in their own projects; much like the package managers of other languages such as Ruby and Python. As a result Microsoft supported an open source project to create a package manager for Visual Studio called the NuGet package manager. NuGet allows developers to download packages of libraries that will install themselves into a project, configure themselves, and then be ready for use by the developer. The package manager also does the work of looking for new updates and applying those updates when they are available.

In this recipe you'll see how to use the NuGet package manager in Visual Studio 2012.

Getting ready

Create a new C# ASP.NET MVC 4 Web Application using the Internet Application project template and give it the default name.

How to do it...

1. In **Solution Explorer,** right-click on the references node for the project and select **Manage NuGet Packages**.

2. The **Manage NuGet Packages** dialog will appear. Ensure the **Online** group is selected on the left side and then in the search box at the top-right enter `coffeebun` and wait a moment for the results.

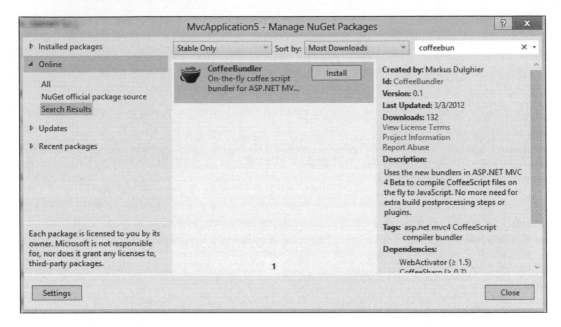

3. Click on the **Install** button to add the `CoffeeBundler` package to your project.

4. Wait for the installation dialog to complete and disappear. You should now see a tick next to the `CoffeeBundler` package, indicating it has been installed.

5. Close the **NuGet** window and then expand the **References** node for the project in **Solution Explorer**. You should see not only the `CoffeeBundler` assembly but also assemblies for other packages that the bundler relies on in the reference list as shown in the following screenshot:

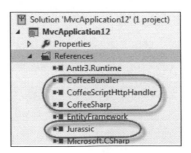

6. Open the NuGet window again by right-clicking on the **References** node and selecting **Manage NuGet Packages**.

7. Over time the packages you have installed will become stale as the package owner releases new and updated versions. In the NuGet package manager select the **Updates** node on the left side of the dialog. Wait a moment to see if there are any available updates.

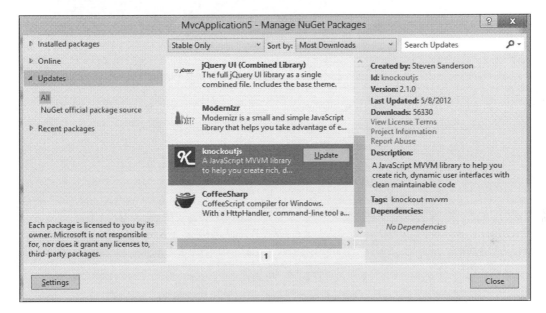

8. In this case there are a number of packages that have updates. Select the **knockoutjs** entry from the list and click on the **Update** button.

9. Wait for the installation dialog to process the update and then disappear. A green tick will appear next to the item indicating the package is now up-to-date. Close the dialog.

10. You should also update the jQuery libraries and any other packages that also have updates. To save you time, instead of updating them one at a time NuGet offers the ability to perform a bulk update.

    From the menu select **View | Other Windows | Package Manager Console**.

11. In the console, enter the text `update-package` and press *Enter*:

```
Package Manager Console
Package source:  NuGet official package source  ▾  ⚙  Default project:  MvcApplication12
licenses. Follow the package source (feed) URL to determine any dependenc

Package Manager Console Host Version 1.8.30423.9026

Type 'get-help NuGet' to see all available NuGet commands.

PM> update-package    ◄─────────
◂
Package Manager Console   Find Results 1
```

12. NuGet will then locate and install updates for all packages automatically. Because package installation in web projects often affects the `Web.config` file you may get prompted to reload it a number of times. Each time you do, just click on **Yes**.

    The results of the update will be shown in the **Package Manager Console**, as shown in the following screenshot:

```
Package Manager Console
Package source:  NuGet official package source  ▾  ⚙  Default project:  MvcApplication12
Updating 'CoffeeSharp' from version '0.3' to '0.5' in project 'MvcApplication12'.
Successfully removed 'CoffeeSharp 0.3' from MvcApplication12.
Successfully installed 'CoffeeSharp 0.5'.
Successfully added 'CoffeeSharp 0.5' to MvcApplication12.
Successfully uninstalled 'CoffeeSharp 0.3'.
No updates available for 'WebActivator' in project 'MvcApplication12'.
No updates available for 'Microsoft.Web.Infrastructure' in project 'MvcApplication12'.

PM>
```

13. Compile and run the application to check that everything still works as expected.

How it works...

NuGet uses a central, well-known location for storing packages located at `http//nuget.org`. Anyone can create and upload packages to this site and the site features a gallery allowing you to search and browse all available packages.

For many people the NuGet site is the first port of call when looking for a package to help them in their development efforts.

There's more...

A lot of organizations build their own utilities, frameworks, and helpers for use in development and share them across various projects.

Managing these dependencies can become difficult over time. Fortunately NuGet can be configured to use local locations for packages, either using a filesystem location or your own internal NuGet server.

 If you wish to host your own NuGet server, instructions can be found at `http://github.com/NuGet/NuGetGallery/wiki/Hosting-the-NuGet-Gallery-Locally-in-IIS.`

To configure Visual Studio to use a local location for NuGet packages, go to **Tools | Options | Package Manager | Package Sources** and add entries by filling in the **Name** and **Source** fields and then clicking on the **Add** button.

The following screenshot shows two extra entries, one configured to point to a local NuGet server and the other pointing to a network share:

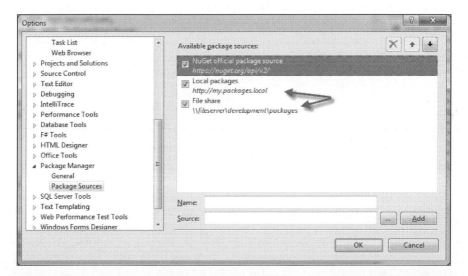

Unit testing .NET applications

When it comes to unit testing, Visual Studio has always been tightly tied to the MSTest framework. The inclusion of a unit test framework inside Visual Studio has been excellent. It has encouraged developers to improve their quality by writing tests to prove code functions as expected. On the flip side, many developers regard MSTest as an inferior unit test framework when compared with other test frameworks such as NUnit, XUnit, MbUnit, et al. The problem stems from the fact that MSTest does so much more than unit testing and as a result suffers from poor speed and bloat. Additionally, its assertion methods are fragmented across multiple classes and it has a cumbersome approach to data-driven tests and expected exceptions. MSTest has also been tied to the release cycle of Visual Studio, so updates have been very slow and it lags behind when compared to the other test frameworks.

Microsoft is ending the tight coupling between Visual Studio and MSTest by making the unit test framework pluggable. MSTest is still provided out of the box but now developers can choose the framework that they like most, on the proviso that their choice of framework implements a Visual Studio adapter.

Microsoft is also removing Test Impact Analysis from Visual Studio (it's still there in Microsoft Test Manager) and replacing it with a Continuous Testing style feature instead. **Continuous Testing** is an approach that has been gaining popularity because of the incredibly rapid feedback cycle it gives developers. The idea is that each time a change is saved in the source files, the unit tests are run to see if anything has broken. This works well with dynamic languages such as Ruby, however as .NET is a static language, this approach is not so simple. In Visual Studio 2012, instead of having all tests run whenever the source is saved, you can have them run automatically each time the code is compiled.

In this recipe, you will use the XUnit testing framework in a test first manner to implement a very simple calculator and you'll see how the Continuous Testing feature works. The important part of this recipe isn't so much the code you will write but in seeing how Visual Studio 2012 can change your development practices when it comes to unit testing. Let's get to it!

Getting ready

Install the **xUnit.net runner for Visual Studio 2012** Visual Studio extension. You can do so via the **Tools | Extensions and Updates** menu option (search for xUnit) or download the .vsix file from the Visual Studio gallery and install it manually (http://visualstudiogallery. msdn.microsoft.com/463c5987-f82b-46c8-a97e-b1cde42b9099).

In Visual Studio 2012, create a new C# Class Library and name it UnitTests.

How to do it...

1. Use NuGet to add the xUnit.net package to your project. See the *Managing packages with NuGet* recipe in this chapter for how to do this.

2. Rename Class1.cs to CalculatorOperations.cs. You will be prompted to rename all references to Class1. Click on **Yes** so that Visual Studio will rename Class1 to CalculatorOperations in the code itself.

3. In the CalculatorOperations class file add the following test method. Don't worry that the code won't compile yet. In a test-driven approach you write the tests first to work out how your code should behave before you implement anything.

```
using Xunit;

namespace UnitTests
{
    public class CalculatorOperations
    {
        [Fact]
        public void Adding_1_and_2_should_give_3()
        {
            var calculator = new Calculator();
            var result = calculator.Add(1, 2);
            Assert.Equal(3, result);
        }
    }
}
```

4. You now need to add a `Calculator` class, but you probably don't want it in your test assembly. Add a new C# class library to the **Unit Test** solution and call it `CalculationEngine`.

5. Rename `Class1.cs` to `Calculator.cs` and, when prompted, allow Visual Studio to rename `Class1` to `Calculator`.

6. Switch back to the `UnitTests` project and add a project reference to the `Calculator` project.

7. Place the cursor on the `Calculator()` constructor call in the unit test and either mouse over and click the actions drop down or press *Ctrl+.* to show the available actions. Select the **using CalculationEngine;** option to add the required `using` statement to your test code.

8. Now place the cursor on the `Add()` method on the next line and bring up the available tasks. Again, do this either by hovering over the code with the mouse and then clicking the options drop down when it appears or by pressing *Ctrl+.* and selecting the only available option to generate the method stub.

9. Open the **Test Explorer** via the **Test | Windows | Test Explorer** menu option.

10. Select the **Run All** option in the **Test Explorer** to compile the code and run the tests in the project for the first time.

11. The unit test should fail at this point because the method stub you generated for the **Add** method simply throws a `NotImplementedException`.

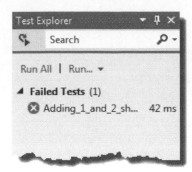

12. Turn on the continuous testing option by either selecting **Test | Test Settings | Run Tests After Build** from the menu or clicking the icon in the top left of the **Test Explorer**.

13. Switch to the `Calculator` class file and implement the `Add()` method by using the code shown in the following screenshot:

```
public class Calculator
{
    public object Add(int p1, int p2)
    {
        return p1 + p2;
    }
}
```

14. Press *Ctrl+Shift+B* to rebuild the solution. Right-clicking the solution and selecting **Build All** will have the same result.

15. Watch the **Test Explorer**. It will automatically rerun the unit tests without you having to do anything. Fantastic!

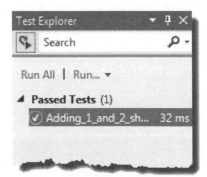

16. To wrap things up, check your code coverage. Click on the **Run** drop-down box in the **Test Explorer** and select **Analyze Code Coverage**.

17. The solution will be recompiled with coverage enabled, the unit tests will be run again, and the results then displayed in the **Code Coverage Results** window as shown in the following screenshot:

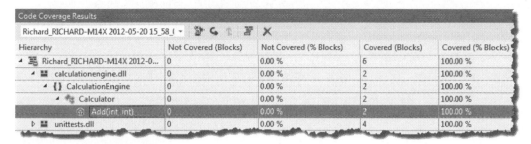

How it works...

Visual Studio no longer needs a special project type for unit tests. The test adapters take care of the discoverability aspects for you. The adapter driven approach has also allowed Microsoft to create a unit test optimized version of MSTest that is fast and light and can be used in standard class libraries without a problem. There is no need for special unit test projects any more, or any of the `.vsmdi` and `.testsettings` files that you're used to.

You can also mix and match your unit test frameworks. It is entirely valid to have MSTest, xUnit, and NUnit tests in one assembly. For example, you may have a suite of older tests in one framework and you want to transition to a new framework without reworking all those old tests. Now you can, without any problem at all.

Out of the box, Visual Studio 2012 only supports the MSTest framework, however adapters are available in the Visual Studio Gallery for the major test frameworks, and the Chutzpah test adapter adds support for both the qUnit and Jasmine JavaScript unit test frameworks.

As mentioned, MSTest no longer requires a `TestSettings` file for unit test projects. If you add a new Unit Test project to your solution you simply get a class library project with a reference already added to `Microsoft.VisualStudio.QualityTools.UnitTestFramework`.

 `TestSettings` files can still be used with MSTest unit test projects, however if they are included, MSTest reverts to Visual Studio 2010 compatibility mode and you will have much slower execution of unit tests.

There's more...

The changes in the test runner are fairly dramatic and with it come a number of other changes you should be aware of.

Can I restrict the unit tests that automatically execute?

In many projects it is common to have unit tests in one test project and integration tests in a second project. Unit tests are considered to be those tests that execute entirely in memory and have no interactions with external systems such as the network, filesystem, screen, or database. Integration tests are those tests that interact with external systems.

If you want to restrict the tests that run so that only unit tests run, and slower integration tests are excluded, you will need to use the **Test Explorer** filter to limit the tests to run. If you have your unit and integration tests in separate assemblies then the **FullName** filter is likely to be the filter that will help you the most.

Asynchronous tests

In .NET 4.5, MSTest now supports asynchronous tests that make use of the `await` keyword.

You can see this in the following code where the method signature is no longer a `public void` method, but rather an async Task:

```
[TestMethod]
async public Task Can_load_Bing_home_page()
{
    var client = new System.Net.WebClient();
    var page = await client.DownloadStringTaskAsync("http://www.bing.com");
    StringAssert.Contains(page, "bing");
}
```

The asynchronous test ensures that the test runner will wait for the test to end before starting the next test. It does not mean that, multiple tests will be run in parallel, just that you can test methods that use async and await.

See also

▶ The *Managing packages with NuGet* recipe

Sharing class libraries across runtimes

There are a number of managed runtimes and profiles for .NET development. These include the normal .NET Framework, Silverlight, XNA, Windows Phone 7, and now the WinRT profile for Windows 8.

If you have to write code that can be shared across more than one of these runtimes it usually involves either the use of copy and paste development (never a good idea!) or multiple versions of the same project and the use of linked files. The linked files approach is cumbersome and error prone and often a pain to work with when Visual Studio is telling you it can't open a file as it is already open in another project.

The solution to this is to use **Portable Class Libraries**. The idea here is that you can build a class library that works across all desired runtimes by ensuring that only code that works on all runtimes is used. Further, the compiler only builds the project once, regardless of the number of runtimes supported, making the overall solution faster to build.

Let's look at a quick example of how a Silverlight application might talk to a .NET application using this approach. To keep the recipe focused we're only going to look at the connection between the two runtimes, not building a full application.

Getting ready

Start Visual Studio 2012 and you're ready to go.

How to do it...

1. Create a **Visual Basic | Silverlight | Silverlight Class Library** project giving it the default name. When you are prompted for the Silverlight version to use, choose **Silverlight 5**.
2. Right-click on the solution and add a **Visual Basic | Class Library** project, again giving it the default name.
3. Right-click on the solution one more time and add a **Visual Basic | Portable Class Library** project, once again giving it the default name.

4. When you are prompted for the **Target Frameworks,** change the selections so that only **.NET Framework 4.5** and **Silverlight 4 and higher** are selected and then click on the **OK** button.

5. Right-click on the Silverlight project in **Solution Explorer** and select **Add Reference**. In the **Reference Manager** dialog, navigate to the **Solution | Projects** node and select the checkbox next to **PortableClassLibrary1**. Click on **OK** to add the reference to the project.

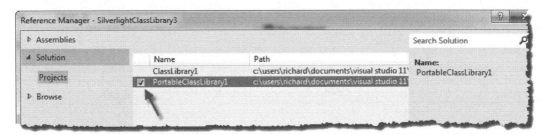

6. In the same way, add a reference to **PortableClassLibrary1** to the .NET class library project. You will get a warning about referencing a project using a different .NET runtime and that you will need to compile the project for IntelliSense to work correctly. Click on **OK** to dismiss the warning.

7. Navigate to `Class1.vb` in the `PortableClassLibrary1` project and add a method to `Class1` as shown in the following screenshot:

```
Public Class Class1
    Public Function SharedMethod() As Integer
        Return 42
    End Function
End Class
```

8. Compile the solution.

9. In `Class1.vb` of `ClassLibrary1` check that you can make a call to the portable library using the code shown in the following screenshot:

```
Public Class Class1
    Public Sub CallPortableCode()
        Dim portable As New PortableClassLibrary1.Class1()
        Dim result = portable.SharedMethod()
    End Sub
End Class
```

10. Navigate to `Class1.vb` in the Silverlight project and add the same code that you used in step 9 to check that a call to the portable library can be made from Silverlight as well.

11. Compile the solution to confirm that there are no compiler errors and prove that you can make calls from both .NET Framework 4.5 code and Silverlight code to a single shared, portable library.

How it works...

The portable libraries themselves are just standard .NET class libraries with restrictions on the framework calls that can be made from within them. The set of calls that can be made is determined by the methods that are supported across all target runtimes selected in the project's properties.

When you write your portable libraries avoid adding references to other libraries. Try and design them as standalone libraries. Since most people tend to use portable library classes for WCF contracts, data transfer objects, or calculation libraries, this is unlikely to be a problem.

Detecting duplicate code

Copy and paste development is generally regarded as a bad practice because bug fixes or enhancements in one area of code have to be repeated in all the other copies of the same code. Not only is this time consuming and tedious, but in large code bases it's very easy to miss a change, leading to bugs and lower overall quality.

In Visual Studio 2012, Microsoft has provided a way to detect duplicate code so that you can take remedial action to clean it up. Fantastic! Let's see how this is done.

Getting ready

Start Visual Studio 2012 and you're ready to go.

How to do it...

1. Create a new C# Class Library project and name it `OriginalLibrary`.

2. Rename `Class1.cs` to `OriginalClass.cs` and allow Visual Studio to rename the class itself when prompted.

3. Add a second C# Class Library to the solution giving it the name **DuplicateLibrary**.

4. Rename `Class1.cs` to `DuplicateClass.cs` and, as in step 2, allow Visual Studio to rename the class itself when prompted.

5. In `OriginalClass`, add the following code:

```
public string StringWithSillyCheckDigit(int x, int y)
{
    if (x <= 0)
        throw new ArgumentOutOfRangeException("x", "must be positive");
    if (y <= 0)
        throw new ArgumentException("I don't like negatives", "y");
    var counter = "";
    for (int i = 0; i < x; i++)
    {
        counter += y;
    }
    var checkDigits = new List<char>() { 'a', 'b', 'c', 'd', 'e' };
    var checkDigit = checkDigits[y % 5];
    counter += checkDigit;
    return counter;
}
```

6. Copy and paste the code you just added into `DuplicateClass`, renaming the method to **DuplicatedCheckDigit**.

7. Rename the parameters in `DuplicatedCheckDigit` to p1 and p2.

8. Rename i to `loop` and `counter` to `outString`. Your duplicated method should now look like the following screenshot:

```
public string DuplicatedCheckDigit(int p1, int p2)
{
    if (p1 <= 0)
        throw new ArgumentOutOfRangeException("x", "must be positive");
    if (p2 <= 0)
        throw new ArgumentException("I don't like negatives", "y");
    var outString = "";
    for (int loop = 0; loop < p1; loop++)
    {
        outString += p2;
    }
    var checkDigits = new List<char>() { 'a', 'b', 'c', 'd', 'e' };
    var checkDigit = checkDigits[p2 % 5];
    outString += checkDigit;
    return outString;
}
```

9. From the Visual Studio menu, select **Analyze | Analyze Solution for Code Clones**. The **Code Clone Analysis Results** window will be displayed and will show you where the duplication exists.

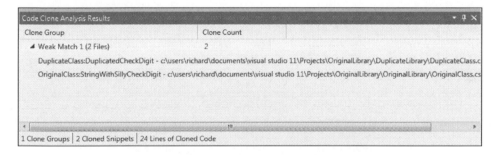

10. Right-click on the **Weak Match 1** result and select **Compare**, as shown in the following screenshot:

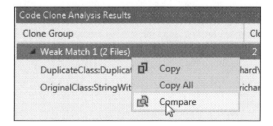

11. The two sections of duplicated code are shown in Visual Studio's new diff viewer and you can decide what remedial action to take from there.

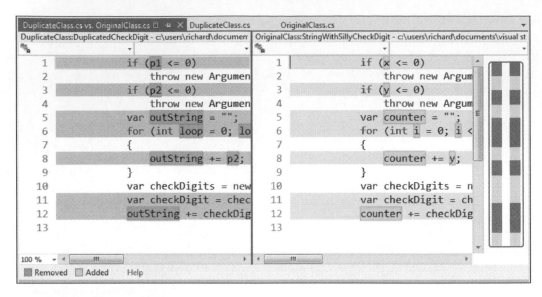

How it works...

You made enough changes in the duplicate method that the code would have been hard to find if you were just using **Find in Files** and looking for variable names or a single line of code. The clone detection algorithm in Visual Studio ignores differences in variable names and instead looks at the structure of the code itself. It also limits searches to duplicates that are a minimum of 10 statements long to prevent detection taking a very long time.

If you do want to search for smaller or specific sections of code you can highlight code in the editor, right-click it and select **Find Matching Clones in Solution**.

There's more...

There are a number of items that get ignored by the detection algorithm to help improve the speed of detection and to exclude files that you are unlikely to be interested in.

Type declarations are ignored. Two classes with the same properties are not considered to be clones, nor are classes with the same method signatures. Only the code within the methods and properties is examined.

The `*.designer.cs` and `*.designer.vb` files are automatically excluded, as is code within any `InitializeComponent` methods.

You can add a `.codeclonesettings` file to your project to exclude certain paths or file types from the comparison. For example, if you are using T4 code generation you may want to place all the generated code in a subfolder and then exclude that folder from the clone detection engine by adding an entry for it in the settings file.

5
Debugging Your .NET Application

In this chapter, we will cover:

- ▶ Debugging on remote machines and tablets
- ▶ Debugging code in production
- ▶ Debugging parallel code
- ▶ Visualizing concurrency

Introduction

It's an unfortunate fact of life, but as developers we occasionally make mistakes and introduce bugs into our code. For some of us it's more than occasionally but we won't talk about that now!

Of course, finding these bugs is easy enough, right? You just run your application and wait for it to blow up. Then it's obvious where the bug is. No? Well then, surely you can run your unit tests and they'll pinpoint the exact line of code that's broken? Hmm, well maybe that's true, but not always. Unfortunately there are a whole range of bugs and problems that are just plain difficult to find without actually debugging your code.

Multi-threaded code and asynchronous code are probably the two most difficult areas for most developers to work with and also the hardest to debug when you have a problem like a **race condition**. A race condition occurs when multiple threads perform an operation at the same time and the order in which they execute makes a difference to how the software runs or the output generated. Race conditions often result in deadlocks, incorrect data being used in other calculations and random, unrepeatable crashes.

The other painful area to debug is code running on other machines, including code in production. Hooking up a remote debugger in previous versions of Visual Studio has been less than simple, and as for debugging code in production the usual response is "are you kidding?"

In this chapter, we're going to see how Visual Studio 2012 improves the debugging experience for these scenarios, and how it can help you diagnose the root cause of a problem faster so you can fix it properly and not just patch over the symptoms.

Debugging on remote machines and tablets

For most developers, debugging an application means setting a breakpoint with *F9* on a line of code, and then pressing *F5* (or **Debug | Start Debugging**) and stepping into and over statements with *F10* and *F11*.

The experience is great when you're debugging code on your local machine, but what if you need to debug code running on a different machine and Visual Studio isn't installed on that machine?

Even though many developers aren't aware of the functionality, debugging code on remote machines with Visual Studio isn't anything new. It's just that until now the debugging experience has been kind of sucky and limited. In Visual Studio 2012 the experience is much improved and combined with speed improvements and an increasing range of devices that applications need to run on, remote debugging is something every developer should know how to do.

This recipe shows you how to configure a machine for remote debugging and then debug an application you have deployed to that machine.

Getting ready

For this recipe you will need a second machine to act as your remote machine. It doesn't matter if it's a virtual or physical machine as long as your development machine and the remote machine can communicate over a network connection.

The recipe assumes that the remote machine doesn't have Visual Studio 2012 installed. The remote machine will need Remote Tools for Visual Studio 2012 installed before starting. If you don't have the Remote Tools already installed, download them from the Microsoft website at `http://go.microsoft.com/fwlink/?linkid=219549` and then install them.

Since you're going to be debugging a .NET application you should also ensure that the .NET Framework 4.5 runtime is installed on the remote machine.

How to do it...

1. Create a new C# console application using the default name.

2. Open the `Program.cs` file and fill in the body of the `Main()` method as shown in the following screenshot:

```csharp
static void Main(string[] args)
{
    Console.ReadKey();   //Wait for keypress to start
    var charCode = 97;
    var outputBuilder = new StringBuilder();
    for (int i = 1; i < 26; i++)
    {
        outputBuilder.Append((char)(charCode + i));
    }
    var output = outputBuilder.ToString();
    Console.WriteLine(output); //Should write "abcd....z"
    Console.ReadKey();
}
```

3. Run the program locally by pressing *F5*. When the console window appears, press any key and you should see a string of characters appear. Press any key again to close the program.

4. It might not be Hello World, but it's certainly close! You should now check if it works on the remote machine. On your remote machine, start the **Remote Debugger Configuration Wizard** and ensure that the **Run the "Visual Studio Remote Debugger" service** checkbox is deselected. Also ensure that the firewall configuration is set as appropriate for your network and then complete the remaining steps of the wizard by taking the default values.

5. Now that you have configured it, start the **Remote Debugger** on your remote machine.

6. When the application appears you should see a message showing the machine name and port number that the debugger is listening on. Take a note of the machine name as you'll be using it later on. In the following screenshot the machine is named **WIN-2008R2** and it is running on port **4016**:

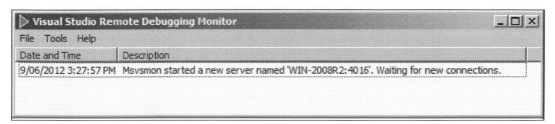

7. For the smoothest development and debugging experience, the remote machine will need to run the code from your development machine via a network share. Either add a specific share to the `bin\debug` folder of your development machine or access it via the inbuilt C$ share. For example, `\\dev-machine\C$\Users\Richard\ Documents\Visual Studio 2012\Projects\ConsoleApplication1\bin\ debug` (your location will vary).

   Ensure that you can connect to your network share from the remote machine.

> Code Access Security is not applied to .NET 4.0 applications by default, but it is for .NET 2.0 applications. To debug a .NET 2.0 application on a remote machine via a file share you need to make sure the share is a trusted location. Use the `caspol.exe` utility in both the x86 and x64 versions of the framework to modify the security settings of your machine. `CasPol. exe -m -pp off -ag 1.2 -url "file://\\server\share\*"` `FullTrust` will set full trust permissions on a file share.

8. In Visual Studio 2012 on your development machine, open the project properties by right-clicking the project in **Solution Explorer** and choosing **Properties**. Select the **Debug** tab.

9. Change the **Start Action** to **Start external program** and enter the path to the compiled application using the path that will be used by the remote machine to start the application. For example, `\\dev-machine\sharename\ ConsoleApplication1.exe`.

10. In the **Start Options** check the **Use remote machine** checkbox and enter the name of the remote machine. This is the machine name you noted in step 6. Your **Debug** tab should now look similar to the following screenshot:

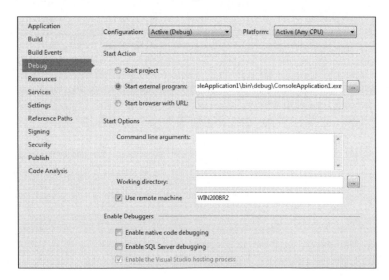

11. On your development machine press *F5* to start debugging. Assuming there are no firewall issues and your permissions are ok, Visual Studio will communicate with the remote machine and launch the application for you automatically.

    Note that, depending on the accounts used on each machine, you may be prompted for login credentials. If that happens, enter the details of the user running the debugging monitor on the remote machine.

 If you have a problem communicating with the remote machine check that the firewall on the remote machine is allowing incoming connections. If it isn't, you can either rerun the Remote Debugger Configuration Wizard to confirm the firewall settings, or manually add a rule to allow a connection on the port number the Remote Debugger is using (the port number is shown in step 6).

12. The application is now waiting for you to press a key. Go back to your development machine and set a breakpoint in the `Main()` method of `Program.cs`, somewhere after the `ReadKey()` method. A good place would be where the `outputBuilder` variable is initialized.

13. Switch back to the remote machine and press a key to continue program execution.

14. Switch back to the development machine. You should find that your breakpoint has been hit and that the application is ready for you to continue debugging.

15. Step through the code in Visual Studio to get a feel of how quick the remote debugging experience is and then continue execution down to the second `Console.ReadKey()` statement. The easiest way to do this, rather than looping through the `for` loop 26 times, is to right-click on the `Console.ReadKey()` statement and select **Run to Cursor**.

16. You may notice that the output has dropped the 'a' at the start of the output string. Is that a display problem or a bug in the code? You can check the string length to be sure. Navigate to the **Immediate Window** and type `?output.Length` to see how long the output string is.

 If the Immediate Window isn't visible you can display it by pressing *Ctrl+Alt+I* or choosing **Debug | Windows | Immediate** from the menu.

17. You should see the value **25** displayed. Note that this value is not from a process on the local machine, it is from the process running on your remote machine. To verify this, select **Debug | Attach to Process** from the menu. In the **Qualifier** drop down, select the remote machine. It will be suffixed by the port number the remote debugger is listening on. When the **Available Process** list is populated you should see **ConsoleApplication1** is the only process on the remote machine that the debugger is attached to.

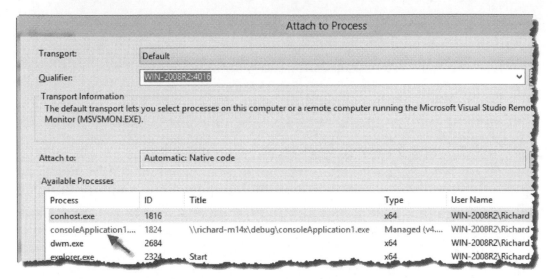

18. Stop debugging by either pressing *Shift+F5*, clicking on the stop button in the debugging toolbar, or choosing **Debug | Stop Debugging** from the menu. This will also terminate the process on the remote machine.

19. Fix the bug in the `for` loop by altering the loop variable to start from 0 instead of 1. Your `for` loop should now look like the code shown in the following screenshot:

```
var outputBuilder = new StringBuilder();
for (int i = 0; i < 26; i++)
{
```

20. Without changing any other setting, press *F5* to start debugging again. Visual Studio will compile the application and launch it on your remote machine for you.

21. Run through the application again to verify that the output is now correct.

How it works...

The main thing to keep in mind when using the remote debugger is that you are looking at data from the remote machine. The debug experience can feel so smooth and so normal that it's easy at times to forget that a path name for a file, for example, is a path relative to the remote machine, not your local machine!

Normally the debugger runs using Windows authentication, however it can be switched over to the "No Authentication" mode. The No Authentication mode enables debugging scenarios for managed and native debugging across versions of Windows that were previously not possible. The danger of this approach is that it opens up a security hole, including allowing attackers to launch any application they choose. Do not run the remote debugger on production machines in this way. The remote debugger is a developer tool and should only be run when developers require it.

There's more...

If you don't want to install the remote debugger on the remote machine, you can run it directly from a file share, however you won't be able to debug Windows Store apps in Windows 8 or debug JavaScript.

Another thing to note is that when you are debugging a Windows Store app on Windows 8 you will not need to change the **Start Action** of the project to start an external program. Leaving it set to **Start project** and then ticking the checkbox and setting the value of the **Use remote machine** field will tell Visual Studio that the project should be packaged and deployed to the remote machine before debugging commences.

Debugging an ASP.NET process

To debug ASP.NET websites running under IIS you do not need to make any changes to the project properties to configure the remote debugger. In fact, you can't. The options aren't available.

For remote debugging you will either need to run the remote debugger as a service or run the application as an administrator. On your development machine you then use the **Attach to Process** dialog to connect to the ASP.NET worker process and begin the debugging session.

To configure the remote debugger as a service, rerun the **Remote Debugger Configuration Wizard** and check the option to run it as a service.

Much like you did in this recipe, for the best debugging experience you should configure the IIS application on the remote machine to run from a network share, pointing to the web application's source folder on your development machine.

Once the web application is running in Visual Studio, select the **Debug | Attach to Process** menu option. The **Qualifier** drop down is the name of the debugger instance you are connected to and this should be the remote machine. If you are unsure of what the machine name is, you can use the **Find** button to locate available debuggers.

Once you are connected to the correct machine, locate the ASP.NET worker process (w3wp) from the list, select **Attach**, and then close the window. You are now connected to the remote debugger for the web application and can set breakpoints in your pages and step through code just as you would expect. Perfect!

I don't want to use a file share

The suggestion to run the programs on the remote machine via a file share is just a tip to make the development process simpler and to eliminate the time it takes to redeploy the application you are trying to debug each time you make a change.

If you don't want to run the application from a file share then you will need to deploy the application to the remote machine and use the **Attach to Process** dialog to connect the debugging session each time.

I'm missing symbols

When debugging remote processes you may find that after you attach to a process and set a breakpoint it will look similar to the following screenshot:

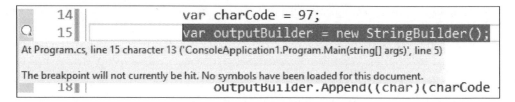

This occurs because Visual Studio either can't load the symbol information (the PDB file) of the executable file or the version that is running on the remote machine is not the same as the one on your development machine (you may have recompiled the code since you last deployed, for example).

Never fear! There's a way to fix this. Follow the given steps:

1. Go to the **Debug | Windows | Modules** menu entry to display the **Modules** window.

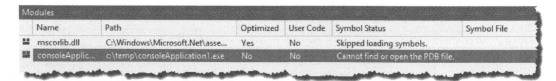

2. Right-click on the entry with the missing symbols and, from the options, choose **Load Symbols From | Symbol Path**.

3. From the file selection dialog box, locate the correct symbol file (PDB file) to load. Once you do this, the debug breakpoints will change to show filled in red dots, as expected, and the **Modules** window will indicate that symbols are loaded.

Debugging code in production

If you're like most people there's nothing more exciting than having a fully-tested application that goes to production and then starts randomly misbehaving for no apparent reason. It's a great way to get the adrenalin going as you rapidly try to figure out what's going wrong from bug reports such as "it just stopped working" and "nothing updated but I don't know why". Wait, what, you don't like that? You're not one of those people? Oh, I see.

Ok, so let's say this does happen to you and your application has random crashes, hangs, misbehaves, and has other bugs. Diagnosing these problems in a production environment can be rather tricky, especially if you are in an environment where you have no production access. This is where **IntelliTrace** can help.

IntelliTrace was introduced in Visual Studio 2010 as a way for developers and testers to record what they'd just done leading up to a bug and then step back through those actions to make diagnosis of the bug simpler. In Visual Studio 2012 this feature has been extended so that system administrators can capture IntelliTrace information from live, running production systems and send the logs to developers for diagnosis.

This recipe will show you how to gather information from a live application running in a production environment and then diagnose and debug problems.

Getting ready

You will need a machine to use as your "production" machine. It doesn't have to be a genuine production machine, just a second machine without Visual Studio installed. A virtual machine is perfectly acceptable.

Your nominated production machine will need to have .NET Framework 4.5, PowerShell and, as you will be diagnosing a web application, Internet Information Server, installed on it.

 If you are really tight for machines and can't even run a virtual machine then you can use your development machine as your "production" server for the purposes of this recipe.

How to do it...

1. On your development machine, create a new application with the default name by selecting **Visual Basic | ASP.NET Web Forms Application**.

2. Open the `default.aspx` page and add a button to the bottom of the page. Give it an ID of **clicky**, set the text attribute to **Click Me!**, and ensure that a button click event is created as shown in the following screenshot:

```
    </p>
        <p><asp:Button ID="clicky" runat="server" OnClick="" ></p>
</asp:Content>
                                                    ⚡ <Create New Event>
                                                    ⚡ Page_Load
```

3. In the code behind file, add code for the button's click event handler as shown in the following screenshot:

```
Protected Sub clicky_Click(sender As Object, e As EventArgs)
    Dim second As Integer = DateTime.Now.Second
    If (second Mod 2 = 0) Then
        Throw New ApplicationException("No clicky for you!")
    Else
        clicky.Text = "current second: " & second.ToString()
    End If
End Sub
```

4. Now when you run the application and click on the button, an exception will be thrown whenever the current time has an even numbered second.

5. Deploy your web application to your production server. Confirm that it runs and that it throws exceptions randomly when the button is clicked.

6. On your production server, create two folders, `c:\IntelliTrace` and `c:\IntelliTraceLogs`. The first will hold the IntelliTrace executables and the second will be where the captured data is placed.

7. Download the IntelliTrace Collector for Visual Studio from `http://go.microsoft.com/fwlink/?LinkId=245688`. Run the executable and, when prompted for the location to place the extracted files, enter `C:\IntelliTrace`.

8. Extract the contents of the `IntelliTraceCollection.cab` file by opening a command prompt, changing directory to the `C:\IntelliTrace` folder, and then typing the following command:

   expand IntelliTraceCollection.cab -F:*.* .

9. You next need to import the IntelliTrace PowerShell module. Open an elevated PowerShell prompt (that is, Run As Administrator), change the directory to `C:\IntelliTrace`, and then enter the following command:

```
Import-Module
.\Microsoft.VisualStudio.IntelliTrace.PowerShell.dll
```

10. To verify that the module was imported correctly and to see the available commandlets, use the following command:

```
Get-Command *intelli*
```

You should see the following output:

11. Before you start the IntelliTrace data collection you need to ensure that the web server can write to the log location. In the production server, start IIS Manager, navigate to your web application, and select **Basic Settings**. Make a note of the name of the **Application pool** being used.

12. Navigate to the **Application Pools** node in IIS Manager and make a note of the **Identity** (that is, the account name) used by the application pool your application is running under; as identified in step 11.

13. Grant the account used by the application pool full access to the `c:\IntelliTraceLogs` location. In **Windows Explorer**, right-click on the folder and select **Properties**. Click on the **Security** tab. If the account is not listed in the **Group or User Names** list, click on the **Edit** button and add the account used by the application pool to the list. If you use the inbuilt **ApplicationPoolIdentity** then you will need to enter the account as `IIS APPPOOL\<Pool Name>` as shown in the following screenshot:

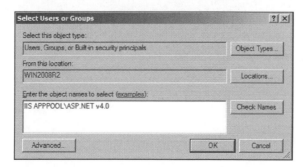

14. Once the account for the application pool is added, ensure that the account has write access to the `c:\IntelliTraceLogs` folder, then click on **OK** to close all the dialogs.

15. Go back to the PowerShell prompt and start collecting IntelliTrace information by entering the following command. Note that the first parameter is the name of the application pool the site is running under and may vary for your web application.

```
Start-IntelliTraceCollection "DefaultAppPool" c:\IntelliTrace\
collection_plan.ASP.NET.trace.xml c:\IntelliTraceLogs
```

16. From your browser, navigate to your web application and click on the button until you have seen both successful and unsuccessful button click events.

17. Once you have enough event information, stop the collection process by going back to the production server, and in the PowerShell prompt enter the following command:

```
Stop-IntelliTraceCollection "DefaultAppPool"
```

An `.iTrace` file will now be present in the `C:\IntelliTraceLogs` folder containing the IntelliTrace logging information that you recorded.

18. Now it's time to see what happened. Copy the `.iTrace` file from the `c:\IntelliTraceLog` folder of your production server to a folder on your local machine.

19. Double-click on the `.iTrace` file to open it in Visual Studio. Alternately, if Visual Studio is already open, you can either press *Ctrl+O* or use the **File | Open | File** menu option to load it. Once the file loads, you should be able to see a **Web Requests** section that looks a little like the following screenshot:

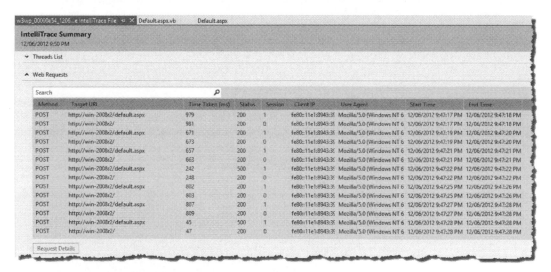

20. In the request list, find a request with a return code of **500**, select it, and then click on the **Request Details** button below the list, as shown in the following screenshot:

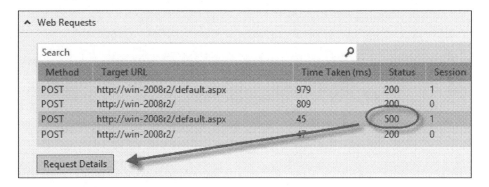

21. The details of the individual request are shown along with the actions that occurred and any exceptions that were thrown:

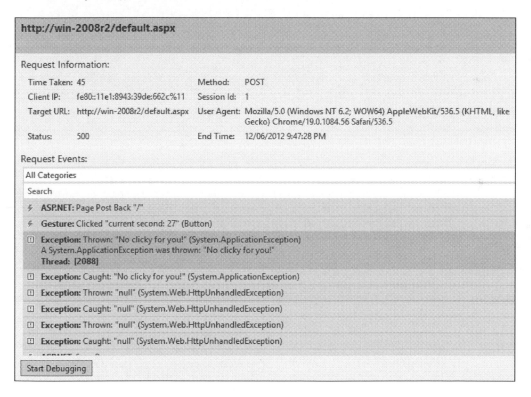

22. Select the entry in the list where the exception is first thrown, as in the screenshot in step 21, and click on the **Start Debugging** button.

23. The code will be displayed and the execution point will be positioned where the exception was thrown:

```
 8    Protected Sub clicky_Click(sender As Object, e As EventArgs)
 9        Dim second As Integer = DateTime.Now.Second
10        If (second Mod 2 = 0) Then
11            Throw New ApplicationException("No clicky for you!")
12        Else
13            clicky.Text = "current second: " & second.ToString()
14        End If
15    End Sub
```

24. You can then use the IntelliTrace debugging controls to move around the code and diagnose what occurred by following the execution path and inspecting parameters.

How it works...

No recompilation of code was required for this to work. The application is untouched and the website didn't need to be restarted. Collecting Intellitrace data is something that your systems administrators can do on your behalf, safe in the knowledge that the application will be unchanged, and that existing web requests will complete normally. This makes debugging and diagnosing those tricky production problems a much more viable prospect.

There's more...

The IntelliTrace settings used in the recipe are the detailed trace settings. They will record execution flow as well as events and will have some impact on production performance. There is a second collection plan provided in the cab file, `collection_plan.ASP.NET. default.xml`, that only records events and therefore has a minimal impact on performance.

Finding errors in large trace files

When there are many requests in the trace you can make it easier to find web requests that have thrown exceptions by using filtering. For example, entering 500 in the **Search** box and clicking on **Filter** would only show requests with a HTTP 500 return code or where 500 appears in the request URL.

Don't forget that IntelliTrace files can get very big, very quickly. Make sure that the location you place them in has plenty of space if you want to capture data over a reasonable time period, and more so if you have a busy production server. Logging to the system drive like we did in the recipe is generally not recommended since filling your system drive will bring your server to a grinding halt.

Where are my variable values?

If you haven't used it before you might expect IntelliTrace to be equivalent to the normal debugging experience. Unfortunately the performance impact of recording all the data needed to simulate the full debugging experience makes this prohibitive.

By default, variable values are not recorded by IntelliTrace unless a breakpoint has been set or an event occurs. In the recipe, if during the debugging session you hovered your mouse over the second variable in the code window, you would see an indication that the data was not collected, as shown in the following screenshot:

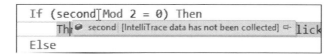

If you wanted to capture that information you could configure IntelliTrace to record tracing information and add trace statements for your code, or you could write custom IntelliTrace events (outside the scope of this book) and add them to the IntelliTrace configuration. In either case it would require recompiling and redeploying code to production. So there is an assumption that you know the level of trace information you will need ahead of time.

Debugging parallel code

With the prevalence of multi-core CPU's we are seeing more and more applications taking advantage of parallel processing to improve performance.

.NET Framework 4.0 added a number of features such as **Task Parallel Library (TPL)** and **Parallel LINQ (PLINQ)** to make developing applications that take advantage of multi-core CPUs much simpler to write.

While the debugging experience for threaded applications in Visual Studio 2010 was good, it gets even better with Visual Studio 2012, and this recipe will show you how to use these improvements.

Getting ready

Start Visual Studio 2012 and create a new C# console application. For this recipe call the application ParallelDebugging.

How to do it...

1. Use the following code to populate the body of `Program.cs`. It's a pretty simple program that starts a parallel `for` loop which, in turn, calls a method that performs meaningless calculations intended to keep the CPU busy.

```
static void Main(string[] args)
{
    Parallel.For(0, 100000, i => SlowMethod(i + 1));
}

private static void SlowMethod(int i)
{
    var total = 0;
    for (int loop = 0; loop < 1000000; loop++)
    {
        total += loop;
        total /= i;
    }
}
```

2. Press *F5* to run the program and after a second or two break into the debugger either by pressing the pause button in Visual Studio or by pressing *Ctrl+Alt+Break*.

3. You will most likely break inside `SlowMethod()`. When you do, you should be able to see the current value of the variable `i` by hovering over the variable name as shown in the following screenshot:

```
var total = 0;
for (int loop = 0; loop < 1000000; loop++)
{
    total += loop;
    total /= i;
}            i  190
```

4. This is standard behavior when debugging however you are only seeing the value of `i` for a single thread. What about the value of `i` on all the other threads? From the menu, select **Debug | Windows | Threads** and you will see all the threads in the application, including the threads the parallel `for` loop has created.

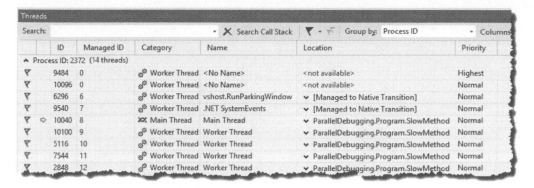

5. Right-click on a different thread from the one you are currently on and select **Switch To Thread** from the context menu. Now look at the values of i, loop, and total and you will see they are different.

6. This is useful but still fairly cumbersome if you want to see the value of i across all threads. For a more holistic view, from the menu, choose **Debug | Windows | Parallel Watch | Parallel Watch 1**. You will see all the current threads listed and an area in the header of the last column for adding watch expressions. Any expression entered will be evaluated across all threads for you automatically.

   Add watch expressions for **i** and **100000-loop** as shown in the following screenshot so you can see how this works:

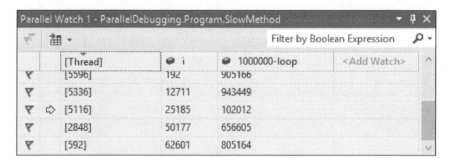

7. Stop debugging. In Visual Studio, add a second console application to the solution named **Parallel2**. In `Program.cs,` use the following code for the body of the file:

```
static void Main(string[] args)
{
    Parallel.For(0, 100000, i => AnotherSlowMethod(i + 1));
}

private static void AnotherSlowMethod(int i)
{
    var total = 0;
    var sb = new StringBuilder(1000 * i);
    for (int loop = 0; loop < 1000 * i; loop++)
    {
        sb.Append(loop);
    }
    total = sb.ToString().Length;
}
```

8. Right-click on the solution in **Solution Explorer** and in the context menu select **Set Startup Projects**. Select **Multiple startup projects** and ensure the **Action** value for both console applications is **Start**.

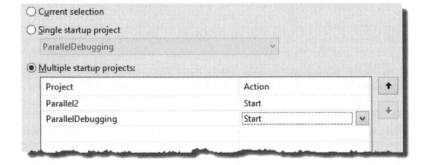

9. Click on **OK** to save the changes and then press *F5* to start debugging.

10. Wait for a short period of time and then break into the debugger using the same process as explained in step 3.

11. From the menu, select **Debug | Windows | Parallel Tasks**. You will see now that you have multiple processes, each with multiple tasks. You can also see what thread each task is running on, as shown in the following screenshot:

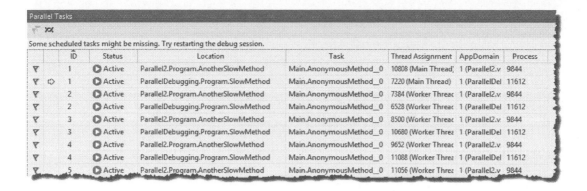

12. From the menu, choose **Debug | Windows | Parallel Stacks**. This view was added in Visual Studio 2010, and in Visual Studio 2012 it was extended to show stacks for multiple processes. As can be seen in the following screenshot, you now have two processes being displayed, each with a main thread and the spawned threads created by the parallel `for` loops of each process.

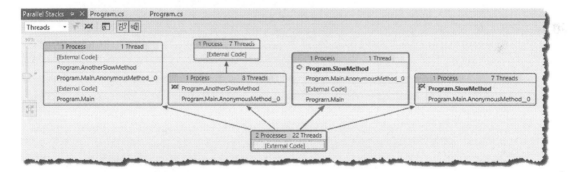

How it works...

Apart from the debugging improvements themselves, Microsoft has worked hard on the Task Parallel Library, PLINQ, and other multi-threading related framework features and gained some serious performance improvements for .NET 4.5. Since .NET 4.5 is an in-place replacement of the .NET 4.0 runtime it means that any of your .NET 4.0 code that uses these libraries will automatically benefit from the performance improvements without you making any recompilation or code changes. Free speed is a good thing!

See also

▶ The *Visualizing concurrency* recipe

Visualizing concurrency

The **Concurrency Visualizer** is another tool that was added in Visual Studio 2010 to assist with multi-threaded code and, just like the other features of Visual Studio related to threading in Visual Studio 2012, it too has been the subject of a number of improvements.

In this recipe, we'll take a look at these improvements and see how you can better understand what is happening inside your application when it runs.

Getting ready

Create a new C# console application named `Concurrency`.

How to do it...

1. Open the `Program.cs` file and add the following statements to the `using` statements at the top of the file:

   ```
   using System.Threading;
   using System.Diagnostics.Tracing;
   ```

2. In the body of `Program.cs` add the following code. It's fairly straightforward. You simply build up a list of tasks you want to run and then you execute them. Each task then calls `SpinWait` on the thread for a period of time. It's much the same as a `Thread.Sleep` method but, instead of the thread yielding back to the operating systems task scheduler, it keeps the CPU busy.

   ```csharp
   static void Main(string[] args)
   {
       var taskList = new List<Task>();
       for (int i = 0; i < 10; i++)
       {
           taskList.Add(Task.Run(() =>
           {
               MyEventSource.Log.RecordAnEvent(DateTime.Now.Second);
               Thread.SpinWait(10000000);
           }));
       }
       Task.WaitAll(taskList.ToArray());
   }
   ```

3. Next add a custom event source as shown in the following screenshot. It will be called whenever a new task is created in the main program loop.

```
[EventSource(Guid = "EE8B671C-90FA-4D6F-A238-F779DBCA6128")]
class MyEventSource : EventSource
{
    internal static MyEventSource Log = new MyEventSource();

    [Event(1)]
    public void RecordAnEvent(int data)
    {
        WriteEvent(1, data);
    }
}
```

4. Launch the **Concurrency Visualizer,** either by pressing the keyboard shortcut of *Alt+Shift+F5,* or from the menu by selecting **Analyze | Concurrency Visualizer | Start With Current Project**.

For the purpose of the recipe, if you are prompted to configure a symbol cache or you see a warning about running without executive paging on an x64 machine you can select **No** in each case.

If you are prompted for elevation then select **Yes** since the collection analyzer requires administrative privileges.

5. When the process completes and the data collection ends you will see a window like the following screenshot:

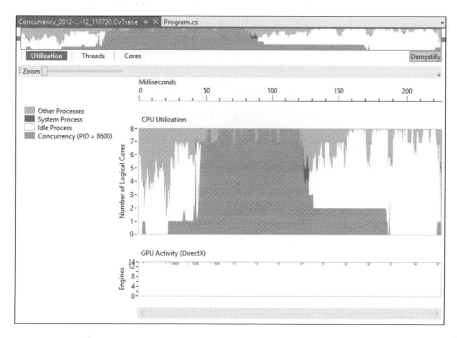

6. At the very top of the window is an overview area with drag handles that you can use to limit the amount of data displayed. Move the red drag handles toward each other so that the selected area contains the high activity area of the trace file.

7. Navigate to the **Threads** view by clicking on the button just under the overview area. You will be shown what has been happening in each thread, but you can also see that your custom event isn't displaying yet. It's high time you sorted that out.

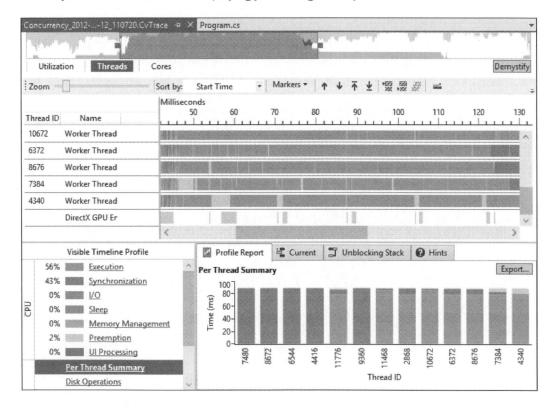

8. Go to the **Analyzer | Concurrency Visualizer | Advanced Settings** menu entry and select the **Markers** tab.

9. Click on the green plus icon to add a new marker. Enter `RecordAnEvent` as the name of the marker and in the **Provider GUID** field enter the GUID you used in the `MyEventSource Event` attribute. The following screenshot shows how this should look. Click on **OK** to close the dialogs.

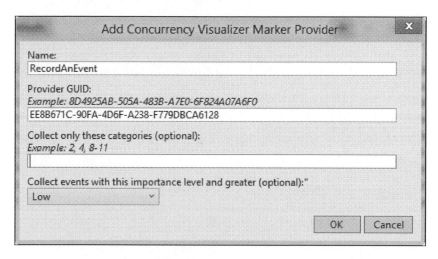

> To make this step a little easier, copy the GUID from the code and paste it into the dialog. It'll help prevent errors when entering the GUID.

10. Repeat step 4 to reanalyze the application and collect updated results, including your newly-added event marker.

11. When the **Concurrency Visualizer** opens, switch to the **Threads** view as before. You should be able to find the custom event information as shown in the following screenshot:

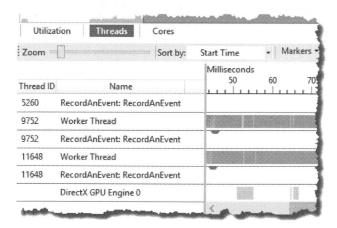

How it works...

The **Concurrency Visualizer** exists to help you understand what the CPU is doing when your application runs and where performance issues may be originating from.

The ability to add your own custom markers is very useful when you want to tie events specific to your application to the visualizer. Apart from custom event data the visualizer also understands the events from the Task Parallel Library, PLINQ, synchronized data structures, and more. This information gives you great insight into your code and will hopefully help you isolate where performance bottlenecks and bugs might be originating from.

See also

▶ The *Debugging parallel code* recipe

6
Asynchrony in .NET

In this chapter, we will cover:

- ▶ Making your code asynchronous
- ▶ Asynchrony and Windows Runtime
- ▶ Asynchrony and web applications
- ▶ Actors and the TPL Dataflow Library

Introduction

Microsoft realized that, while most developers understand the benefits of asynchronous code and the improvements it can bring about in their applications, the programming models involved in asynchrony were fairly cumbersome, verbose and in some cases quite difficult to get right. As a result most developers ignored asynchrony unless circumstances forced it upon them. The extra complexity, effort, time, chance for bugs, and difficulty in debugging meant that it simply wasn't worth it for most developers.

To ensure reading and writing asynchronous code is no longer restricted to only the superhuman amongst us, Visual Studio 2012 and .NET 4.5 introduced the async and await keywords for both the C# and Visual Basic languages. Keywords make asynchronous code as easy to read, write, and debug as normal synchronous code.

As you saw in Chapter 5, Debugging Your .NET Application, the debugging experience is greatly improved in multi-threaded asynchronous code, and now with .NET 4.5 the language support is present to make the development of asynchronous code so easy that there is no excuse for not using it.

In this chapter, you'll be looking specifically at the async and await keywords and seeing how Visual Studio 2012 supports them.

Making your code asynchronous

So you've got yourself an application that might be lacking in the performance department. If you're honest, it's probably horribly slow, and yet when you look at the performance counters on the machine it doesn't seem to be doing all that much. What are the odds that your code is doing a slow operation and blocking the execution thread, preventing other code from executing? Pretty high, huh?

It gets even worse in web applications that come under heavy load. Every request thread that gets blocked is a point where other requests can get queued, and before too long you've got yourself a server that is throwing 503 Service Unavailable errors.

Time to take that synchronous code, stick an "a" on the front of it and make your system start to sing.

Just remember that before you make all of your code asynchronous, you should understand where it blocks and where it doesn't. The overhead of threading can actually make your application run slower if you aren't careful. Now with that in mind, let's go and make some asynchronous code.

Getting ready

You will need an Internet connection for this recipe to work since you load data from various RSS feeds and display it.

Ensure you have a connection, then simply start Visual Studio 2012 and you're ready to go.

How to do it...

Perform the following steps:

1. Create a C# Console Application named `FeedReader`. This application will read the feeds from a number of sites and display them on the console. At the end of the display, the total time required for the feeds to be fetched and displayed will be shown.

2. In the program, classes from a number of different namespaces will be used. To save some time, add the following code to the `using` statements at the top of `Program.cs`:

```
using System.Diagnostics;
using System.Net;
using System.Net.Cache;
using System.Xml.Linq;
```

3. Before you implement the main method, you need to create some supporting methods. Add a `ReadFeed()` private method, as shown after the `Main()` method. It creates a web client to read an RSS feed with the cache setting turned off. This will ensure that we always pull data from the Internet and not a local cached copy.

```
private static string ReadFeed(string url)
{
    var client = new WebClient()
    {
        CachePolicy = new RequestCachePolicy(RequestCacheLevel.NoCacheNoStore)
    };
    var contents = client.DownloadString(url);
    return contents;
}
```

4. Add a `PublishedDate()` method below the `ReadFeed()` method. It will convert dates in the feed, that `System.DateTime` doesn't handle, into dates that can be parsed.

```
public static DateTime PublishedDate(XElement item)
{
    var s = (string)item.Element("pubDate");
    s = s.Replace("EST", "-0500");
    s = s.Replace("EDT", "-0400");
    s = s.Replace("CST", "-0600");
    s = s.Replace("CDT", "-0500");
    s = s.Replace("MST", "-0700");
    s = s.Replace("MDT", "-0600");
    s = s.Replace("PST", "-0800");
    s = s.Replace("PDT", "-0700");
    DateTime d;
    if (DateTime.TryParse(s, out d)) return d;
    return DateTime.MinValue;
}
```

5. Now move back into the `Main()` method and create a variable for the list of feeds to read from.

```
static void Main(string[] args)
{
    var feedUrls = new List<string>(){
        "http://massively.joystiq.com/rss.xml",
        "http://feeds2.feedburner.com/alvinashcraft",
        "http://blogs.msdn.com/b/pfxteam/rss.aspx",
        "http://feeds.feedburner.com/ScottHanselman",
    };
}
```

6. Next create a `Stopwatch` so that you can start timing how long the execution takes, and then add the code to load the data from the feeds.

```
var stopwatch = Stopwatch.StartNew();
var feeds = (from url in feedUrls
             select ReadFeed(url))
            .ToArray();
```

7. You need to parse the feed so you can extract something to show on screen. Add the following code in the `Main()` method, to do so:

```
var items = from feed in feeds
            from channel in XElement.Parse(feed).Elements("channel")
            from item in channel.Elements("item").Take(1)
            let date = PublishedDate(item)
            orderby date descending
            select new
            {
                Title = (string)channel.Element("title"),
                Link = (string)channel.Element("link"),
                PostTitle = (string)item.Element("title"),
                PostLink = (string)item.Element("link"),
                Date = date
            };
```

8. Now, tie a bow around it and finish the program. Complete the `Main()` method by adding the following code to display an item from each feed on the console and show the total time it took to process all feeds:

```
foreach (var item in items)
{
    Console.WriteLine("Title: {0} [{1}]", item.Title, item.Link);
    Console.WriteLine("  Post: {0} [{1}]", item.PostTitle, item.PostLink);
    Console.WriteLine("  Date: " + item.Date);
    Console.WriteLine("---------");
}

Console.WriteLine("Total Time: " + stopwatch.Elapsed);
Console.ReadKey();
```

9. Compile the program and check that it runs. Don't panic if the console takes a little while to show some text, you've got some slow code running here. When it does eventually complete you should see output similar to the following screenshot:

10. Ok, so it's not the fastest code in the world. Time to introduce the `await` and `async` keywords and see if you can't speed this thing up.

    First, locate the `ReadFeed()` method and change the return type from `string` to `Task<string>`.

11. You will then need to return a `Task<string>` object from the method, but you can't just cast the `contents` variable to that type. Fortunately, the `WebClient` class includes a task based version of `DownloadString` called `DownloadStringTaskAsync` that returns a `Task<string>`. Perfect for your needs. Change the code to use `client.DownloadStringTaskAsync(url)`.

```
private static Task<string> ReadFeed(string url)
{
    var client = new WebClient()
    {
        CachePolicy = new RequestCachePolicy(RequestCacheLevel.NoCacheNoStore)
    };
    var contents = client.DownloadStringTaskAsync(url);
    return contents;
}
```

12. Navigate back up to the `Main()` method and you will see a problem with the `Parse()` method in the LINQ statement. The root cause is that the `feeds` variable is now an array of the `Task<string>` objects, and not `string` objects.

13. Change the code where `feeds` is assigned to wrap the LINQ statement in a `Task.WhenAll()` call instead of using `.ToArray()`. The `Task.WhenAll` method creates a task that waits until all of the inner tasks returned by the enclosed LINQ statement are complete. The `await` keyword tells the compiler that the task should be executed asynchronously and the result assigned to the `feeds` variable.

```
var feeds = await Task.WhenAll(from url in feedUrls
                select ReadFeed(url));
```

14. There is still a problem. The compiler is now complaining about the `await` keyword not being valid. Any method where the `await` keyword is used must have the `async` keyword in its declaration. Go to the declaration of the `Main()` method and add the `async` keyword as shown in the following screenshot:

```
static async void Main(string[] args)
{
```

15. Compile the application. You will get an error indicating the `Main` method can't be made asynchronous as it is the program entry point.

16. This is easy enough to work around. Simply rename the `Main()` method to `ProcessFeedsAsync()` and insert a new `Main()` method above it, using the code shown in the following screenshot. Also, remove the `ReadKey()` method from the end of the `ProcessFeedsAsync()` method so that you are not prompted for user input twice.

```
static void Main(string[] args)
{
    Console.WriteLine("starting...");
    ProcessFeedsAsync();
    Console.WriteLine("finished...");
    Console.ReadKey();
}

static async void ProcessFeedsAsync()
{
    var feedUrls = new List<string>(){
    -----------------
    Console.WriteLine("Total Time: " + stopwatch.Elapsed);
    Console.ReadKey();    Delete this line
}
```

17. Compile and run the program. You should see output somewhat similar to the following screenshot and the elapsed time should be shorter than before:

```
file:///C:/Users/Richard/documents/visual studio 11/Projects/FeedReader/FeedReader/bin/Debug/...
starting...
finished...
Title: Parallel Programming with .NET [http://blogs.msdn.com/b/pfxteam/]
    Post: Building Async Coordination Primitives, Part 4: AsyncBarrier [http://bl
ogs.msdn.com/b/pfxteam/archive/2012/02/11/10266932.aspx]
    Date: 12/02/2012 5:59:30 PM
---------
Title: Massively [http://massively.joystiq.com]
    Post: Lime Odyssey dev blog features the music of Yasunori Mitsuda [http://ma
ssively.joystiq.com/2012/02/11/lime-odyssey-dev-blog-features-the-music-of-yasun
ori-mitsuda/]
    Date: 12/02/2012 10:00:00 AM
---------
Title: Scott Hanselman [http://www.hanselman.com/blog/]
    Post: It's 2012 and your kids have an iPhone - Do you know where they are? I
do. [http://feedproxy.google.com/~r/ScottHanselman/~3/CJcTRLucu-4/Its2012AndYour
KidsHaveAnIPhoneDoYouKnowWhereTheyAreIDo.aspx]
    Date: 11/02/2012 3:01:16 PM
---------
Title: Alvin Ashcraft's Morning Dew [http://www.alvinashcraft.com]
    Post: Dew Drop â?" February 10, 2012 (#1,263) [http://feedproxy.google.com/~r
/alvinashcraft/~3/ax5EDZcOGoQ/]
    Date: 10/02/2012 11:57:54 PM
---------
Total Time: 00:00:05.7963579  ◄━━━━━━━━
```

How it works...

As you've seen, Visual Studio offers enough warnings and errors through IntelliSense to make conversion of synchronous code to asynchronous reasonably straightforward, as long as you make changes in small, incremental steps. Large scale changes of code, regardless of what those changes may be, are always difficult and error prone, especially if you lack unit tests or other mechanisms to verify your changes haven't broken any functionality.

The `DownloadStringTaskAsync()` method shows off an important convention to be aware of in the .NET 4.5 Framework design. There is a naming convention to help you to locate the asynchronous versions of methods, where methods that are asynchronous all have an "Async" suffix on their names. In situations where an asynchronous method exists from previous framework versions the newer, task-based, asynchronous methods are named with the "TaskAsync" suffix instead.

In step 16, the `ReadKey()` method was added to stop the main method from completing immediately and terminating the program before any output was returned. In the console window you can see that the **starting** and **finishing** messages are displayed before any of the feed details appear. This occurs because the `ProcessFeedsAsync` method was being executed asynchronously on a separate thread, while the `Main()` method was still being executed on the main application thread. This is exactly what we would expect from non-blocking, asynchronous code.

There's more...

It's possible to overdo it. Every piece of asynchronous code comes with a certain amount of overhead. There is a CPU cost to context switching and a higher memory footprint needed for maintaining memory state for each thread, and if you have too many threads you can actually reduce the performance of your application.

The design guideline for the Windows Runtime libraries in Windows 8 was that any method that was likely to take more than 50 ms to complete was to be made asynchronous; there was a minimum duration used as a way of determining when it made sense to go asynchronous. 50 ms is probably a good final target for your methods as well, but before you go and improve all the methods in your application, start by determining which of your current methods are the slowest. These should be what you target first. Start by improving only methods that take more than 500 ms to complete and resolve those first, before targeting the faster methods.

Whenever determining the appropriate balance between synchronous and asynchronous code, you should be doing performance and load testing on your application to determine what the current performance profile is, and what effect your changes will have on it. Because each and every application is different, finding the right mix can be an art. As a tip, identify the slowest areas of your application and target them first. As you improve performance, keep an eye on how much time it costs you to make your code asynchronous versus the improvement you are seeing in the overall application performance.

Asynchrony and Windows Runtime

When developing the Windows Runtime for Windows 8, Microsoft followed a design guideline where any synchronous method that might take longer than 50 ms to complete was to be removed and replaced with an asynchronous version. The goal behind this design decision is to dramatically improve the chances of developers building applications that feel smooth and fluid by not blocking threads on framework calls.

In this recipe you're going to load the RSS feed details again, just as you did in the *Making your code asynchronous* recipe, though this time you're going to be creating a Windows Store application.

There are a few differences between a Windows Store application and a console one, including differences in the classes available. For example, the `WebClient` class doesn't exist in WinRT so you'll be using the `HttpClient` class instead.

For variety, you will be writing this code using Visual Basic.

Getting ready

Ensure you are running Windows 8 and then launch Visual Studio 2012.

How to do it...

Perform the following steps:

1. Create a new project by selecting **Visual Basic | Windows Store | Blank App (XAML)** and name it `FeedReader`.

2. Add a class named `Post` to the application using the following code. This class will hold the details of each post from the RSS feed that we will show on screen.

```
Public Class Post
    Public Property Title As String
    Public Property Link As String
    Public Property PostTitle As String
    Public Property PostLink As String
    Public Property PostDate As DateTime
End Class
```

3. Open `MainPage.xaml` and add the following XAML to the `<Grid />` element to define the markup of how the results should appear. The layout consists of a button to start the feed loading and a `ListBox` element in which the results are displayed. You also have a `TextBlock` element in which you'll post the time it takes to read the feeds.

```xml
<Grid Background="{StaticResource ApplicationPageBackgroundThemeBrush}">
    <Button Name="LoadFeeds" Margin="116,60,0,0" VerticalAlignment="Top">
        Load Feeds
    </Button>
    <TextBlock Name="TimeTaken" HorizontalAlignment="Left"
        Height="36" Margin="257,60,0,0" TextWrapping="Wrap"
        VerticalAlignment="Top" Width="360" FontSize="32">
        Waiting for click...
    </TextBlock>
    <ListBox Height="450" HorizontalAlignment="Left"
        Margin="116,140,0,0" Name="PostsListBox"
        VerticalAlignment="Top" Width="500" >
        <ListBox.ItemTemplate>
            <DataTemplate>
                <StackPanel Orientation="Vertical" Height="110">
                    <TextBlock Text="{Binding Title}" />
                    <TextBlock Text="{Binding Link}" />
                    <TextBlock Text="{Binding PostTitle}" />
                    <TextBlock Text="{Binding PostLink}" />
                    <TextBlock Text="{Binding PostDate}" />
                </StackPanel>
            </DataTemplate>
        </ListBox.ItemTemplate>
    </ListBox>
</Grid>
```

4. Next, navigate to the code behind file `MainPage.xaml.vb`, and add a couple of imports statements that you will need for later:

```vb
Imports System.Net.Http
Imports System.Net.Http.Headers
```

5. Now add some initial code to define the RSS feeds to use and a collection to hold the `Post` objects.

```vb
Public NotInheritable Class MainPage

    Public Property Posts As List(Of Post)
    Dim feedUrls As New List(Of String)

    Public Sub New()
        InitializeComponent()
        feedUrls = New List(Of String) From {
                "http://massively.joystiq.com/rss.xml",
                "http://feeds2.feedburner.com/alvinashcraft",
                "http://blogs.msdn.com/b/pfxteam/rss.aspx",
                "http://feeds.feedburner.com/ScottHanselman"
        }
        Posts = New List(Of Post)
    End Sub
End Class
```

6. Add the `PublishedDate()` helper method to the class after the `New()` method.

```vb
Public Function PublishedDate(item As XElement) As DateTime
    Dim s As String = CType(item.Element("pubDate"), String)
    s = s.Replace("EST", "-0500")
    s = s.Replace("EDT", "-0400")
    s = s.Replace("CST", "-0600")
    s = s.Replace("CDT", "-0500")
    s = s.Replace("MST", "-0700")
    s = s.Replace("MDT", "-0600")
    s = s.Replace("PST", "-0800")
    s = s.Replace("PDT", "-0700")
    Dim d As DateTime
    If DateTime.TryParse(s, d) Then
        Return d
    End If
    Return DateTime.MinValue
End Function
```

7. Add the `ReadFeed()` helper method below the `PublishedDate()` method using the following code:

```vbnet
Private Async Function ReadFeed(url As String) As Task(Of String)
    Dim client As New HttpClient
    Dim cacheControl As New CacheControlHeaderValue With {
        .NoCache = True,
        .NoStore = True
    }
    client.DefaultRequestHeaders.CacheControl = cacheControl
    client.MaxResponseContentBufferSize = Integer.MaxValue
    Dim response As HttpResponseMessage = Await client.GetAsync(url)
    Dim content As String = Await response.Content.ReadAsStringAsync()

    Dim _posts = From channel In XElement.Parse(content).Elements("channel")
        From item In channel.Elements("item").Take(1)
        Let _date = PublishedDate(item)
        Order By _date Descending
        Select New Post With {
            .Title = CType(channel.Element("title"), String),
            .Link = CType(channel.Element("link"), String),
            .PostTitle = CType(item.Element("title"), String),
            .PostLink = CType(item.Element("link"), String),
            .PostDate = _date
        }
    Dim post = _posts.First
    Posts.Add(post)
    Return ""
End Function
```

8. It's now time to add some functionality to the button that loads the feeds. Write a handler for the `LoadFeeds` button's click event using the following code:

```vbnet
Private Async Sub LoadFeeds_Click(sender As Object, _
                                  e As RoutedEventArgs) _
                        Handles LoadFeeds.Click
    Dim _stopwatch = Stopwatch.StartNew
    Await Task.WhenAll(From url In feedUrls Select ReadFeed(url))
    Dim _timespan As TimeSpan = _stopwatch.Elapsed
    TimeTaken.Text = _timespan.ToString
    PostsListBox.ItemsSource = Posts
End Sub
```

9. Compile and run the program. When the UI appears click on the **Load Feeds** button, wait a few seconds and you should see the results of your work appear as in the following screenshot:

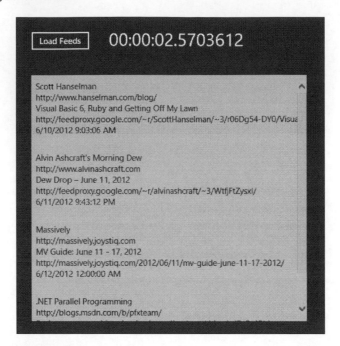

How it works...

In step 8 you added a `LoadFeeds.Click` event handler. The important thing to note about this method is that it is an `async` method and that `await` is used with the `Task.WhenAll` method. When the application runs and you click on the button, the click event fires the event handler, which in turn starts the background processing that reads the feeds. While the application is waiting for that background process to complete, control is returned to the main application for any other work that needs to be done, ensuring you do not block the application while waiting for the feeds to be retrieved. When the feed retrieval completes, execution returns back to the click event handler, which then updates the UI with the results.

In step 7 the `ReadFeed()` method looks similar to what you used in the console application in the *Making your code asynchronous* recipe, however you will now see that you are using the `HttpClient` class instead of the `WebClient` class as it isn't available in the Windows Runtime. The `HttpClient` class also requires different code to set up the cache control values and you have to specify the response buffer size, otherwise you can get runtime exceptions on long feeds.

Since this is a Windows Store app and you are coding against WinRT and the .NET Framework 4.5 Windows Store app profile you cannot produce a synchronous version of the application. The synchronous API calls that you might have used with a console or WPF application simply aren't available.

This makes the `await` and `async` keywords critical for Windows Store apps. Get used to them, know them, love them; even send them thank you cards! Without these keywords, developing asynchronous applications that meet modern design guidelines would be so much harder to do and so much more fragile and difficult to debug. These two little keywords make asynchronous programming very, very simple.

See also

▸ The *Making your code asynchronous* recipe

Asynchrony and web applications

Web applications don't need to be asynchronous, do they? IIS gives each request its own thread so people don't need to worry about it, right? Even if one request goes slow, all the others will still be processed quickly so it's not really a problem, right?

It's surprising how many times this is said by developers, often the same ones who have slow sites even though they have small user loads and few requests per second. If you want a responsive, scalable web application that supports hundreds or thousands of users per server, you need to make the best use of the hardware you are on and you must consider the problems that are caused by blocking threads.

IIS has limits on the number of requests and I/O threads it uses. Blocking any of these threads means IIS is forced to wait until the thread is released before another request can be processed. When there are no threads available to process requests (because of blocking or high-server load), requests start to queue up and, over time, that queue can grow until it reaches its maximum size, at which point the dreaded *503 Service Unavailable* message will start showing to your site's visitors. Not really what you want.

High-server load due to a large volume of visitors is not something you can control. What is in your control, however, is your ability to write code that doesn't block threads and allows IIS to scale and process more requests than would have been possible otherwise.

Once again, you'll use the feed reader scenario, but for simplicity you'll just make the network calls to retrieve the RSS feeds and then display the time it took to do so.

We're not going to cover load testing the site in this recipe since it's a feature that's been around in Visual Studio for quite some time now. See `http://msdn.microsoft.com/en-us/library/dd293540.aspx` for more information on the load testing features in Visual Studio.

Getting ready

Simply start Visual Studio 2012 and you're ready to go.

How to do it...

Create an asynchronous web application by following these steps:

1. Start a new **ASP.NET Empty Web Application** project using C# and give it the default name.

2. Add a new **Web Form** item to the project, leaving it with the default name, which should be the very creative `WebForm1`.

3. In `WebForm1.aspx` add `async="true"` to the end of the page directive. This tells ASP.NET to allow the page lifecycle events prior to the PreRender event to execute asynchronous tasks.

```
<%@ Page Language="C#" AutoEventWireup="true"
    CodeBehind="WebForm1.aspx.cs"
    Inherits="WebApplication10.WebForm1"
    Async="true" %>
```

4. Further down in the page body add an `id` attribute to the `<div>` element and a `runat="server"` attribute so that you can place the timing results in it when the page executes.

```
<form id="form1" runat="server">
<div id="timeTaken" runat="server">

</div>
```

5. Now navigate to the `WebForm1.aspx.cs` code behind file and add some supporting `using` statements as follows:

```
using System.Diagnostics;
using System.Threading.Tasks;
using System.Net;
using System.Net.Cache;
```

6. Next add the supporting `ReadFeed()` method to read a single RSS feed.

```
private async static Task<string> ReadFeed(string url)
{
    var client = new WebClient() {
        CachePolicy = new RequestCachePolicy(RequestCacheLevel.NoCacheNoStore)
    };
    return await client.DownloadStringTaskAsync(url);
}
```

7. Now that you have the `ReadFeed()` method implemented, you should implement the `Page_Init()` method to read all the feed information during page startup. Because you want the page to load asynchronously you will need to register a `PageAsyncTask` object. This lets ASP.NET know that you are performing an asynchronous operation, which is important since page lifecycle events themselves are not asynchronous and without them the page would render before your tasks were complete.

```
private TimeSpan duration;

protected void Page_Init(object sender, EventArgs e)
{
    var feedUrls = new List<string>() {
        "http://massively.joystiq.com/rss.xml",
        "http://feeds2.feedburner.com/alvinashcraft",
        "http://blogs.msdn.com/b/pfxteam/rss.aspx",
        "http://feeds.feedburner.com/ScottHanselman"
    };
    RegisterAsyncTask(new PageAsyncTask(async (ct) =>
    {
        var stopwatch = Stopwatch.StartNew();
        var feeds = await Task.WhenAll(
            from url in feedUrls select ReadFeed(url));
        foreach (var feed in feeds)
        {
            Debug.WriteLine(feed.Length);
        }
        duration = stopwatch.Elapsed;
        timeTaken.InnerText = duration.ToString();
    }));
}
```

8. Finally, add code to the `Page_PreRender()` method so that the duration of the entire page lifecycle, inclusive of the RSS reading, can be seen in the debug console in Visual Studio.

```
protected void Page_PreRender(object sender, EventArgs e)
{
    Debug.WriteLine("Duration: {0}", duration);
}
```

9. Press *F5* to start debugging the application. After a few seconds the page load should complete and render a screen similar to the following screenshot:

10. Leaving the page open, switch back to Visual Studio which should still be in debug mode. Look at the contents of the **Output** window and the **Debug** messages in particular. As shown in the following screenshot, you should see that the debug message from the `PreRender` event is displayed before the four numbers, showing the size of data pulled from the RSS feeds.

The duration shows as zero because the `Page_Init` method has completed, but `PageAsyncTask` you registered has not yet executed by the time the `PreRender` method is called.

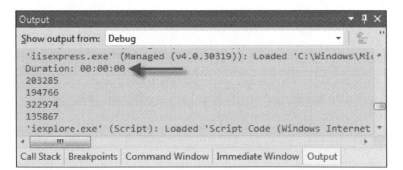

How it works...

It's important to keep in mind that with ASP.NET Web Forms the page methods are executed synchronously, even if you put the `async` keyword on the method declarations. You must use `RegisterAsyncTask`, just as you needed to in previous .NET versions.

Because of the `async` keyword, the registering of tasks is now simply a matter of including a lambda in the code. You don't need to follow the old style of asynchronous programming anymore and you don't have to write any begin and end methods for the framework to call.

You will also notice that the page itself still took a while to load. The asynchronous approach you used allows the web server as a whole to scale and process more requests concurrently. It doesn't magically make those slow network calls to the RSS feeds any faster, so be prepared to think of other ways to improve your user interface to indicate to your users that something is happening and to just be patient.

There's more...

You may be thinking "what about ASP.NET MVC 4?". Well, in ASP.NET MVC 4, things are even simpler.

Your controller still inherits from the `AsyncController` class, however, instead of having to write method pairs for the beginning and ending of an asynchronous operation, you simply have to create a controller method that returns a `Task<T>`.

For example:

```
public async Task<ActionResult> Index()
{
    await LongRunningMethod();
    return View();
}
```

This is much better than how asynchronous controllers worked in previous versions of ASP. NET MVC. It's now so easy!

See also

 ▸ The *Making your code asynchronous* recipe

Actors and the TPL Dataflow Library

With Visual Studio 2010 and .NET 4.0 we were given the **Task Parallel Library (TPL)**, which allowed us to process a known set of data or operations over multiple threads using constructs like the `Parallel.For` loop.

Coinciding with the release of Visual Studio 2012, Microsoft has now given us the ability to take any data we like and process it in chunks through a series of steps, where each step can be processed independently of the others. This library is called the **TPL Dataflow Library**.

An interesting thing to note about this library is that it was originally included as part of .NET Framework in the pre-release versions, but the team moved it to a NuGet distribution model so that changes and updates to the package could be made outside of the normal .NET lifecycle. A similar approach has been taken with the **Managed Extensibility Framework (MEF)** for web and Windows Store apps. This change to the distribution model shows a willingness from Microsoft to change their practices so that they can be more responsive to developer needs.

From a terminology perspective, the processing steps are called **Actors** because they "act" on the data they are presented with and the series of steps performed are typically referred to as a **pipeline**.

A fairly common example of this is in image processing where a set of images needs to be converted in some way, such as adding sepia tones, ensuring all images are in portrait mode, or doing facial recognition. Another scenario might be taking streaming data, such as sensor feeds, and processing that to determine actions to take.

This recipe will show you how the library works. However, to keep things short, we won't do any fancy image processing. Instead, we'll just take some keyboard input and display it back on the screen after having converted it to uppercase and Base64 encoding it.

In order to do this we will use an `ActionBlock` object and a `TransformBlock` object. An `ActionBlock` object takes a piece of data passed to it and does something with it, that is, it performs an action using it, and a `TransformBlock` object takes a piece of data and changes it in some way.

In this recipe, you will use a `TransformBlock` object to convert characters to uppercase and encode them before passing them to an `ActionBlock` object to display them on screen.

Getting ready

Simply start Visual Studio 2012 and you're ready to go.

How to do it...

Create a DataFlow powered application using the following steps:

1. Create a new application targeting .NET Framework 4.5 by selecting **Visual C# | Console Application** and name it `DataFlow`.

2. Using NuGet, add the `TPL Dataflow` library to the project.

3. Open `Program.cs` and at the top of the file add the following `using` statements:

```
using System.Threading;
using System.Threading.Tasks;
using System.Threading.Tasks.Dataflow;
```

4. In the `Main()` method of `Program.cs` add the following code to define the `ActionBlock`. The method in the `ActionBlock` object displays a `String` on the console and has a `Sleep` method call in it to simulate long running work. This gives you a way to slow down processing and force data to be queued between steps in the pipeline.

```
var slowDisplay = new ActionBlock<string>(async s =>
    {
        await Task.Run(() => Thread.Sleep(1000));
        Console.WriteLine(s);
    }
    , new ExecutionDataflowBlockOptions { MaxDegreeOfParallelism = 4 }
);
```

5. Next, add the code for `TransformBlock`. The `TransformBlock` object will take a `char` as input and return an uppercase base64 encoded `string`. The `TransformBlock` object is also linked to the `ActionBlock` object to create a two-step pipeline.

```
var transformer = new TransformBlock<char, string>(c =>
{
    var upper = c.ToString().ToUpperInvariant();
    var bytes = ASCIIEncoding.ASCII.GetBytes(upper);
    var output = Convert.ToBase64String(bytes);
    return output;
});
transformer.LinkTo(slowDisplay);
```

6. Now add code to take input from the console and pass it to the first step of the pipeline (the `TransformBlock` object in this case). You also need to close and flush the pipeline when you hit *Enter* so that you can exit the program.

```
bool keepGoing = true;
while (keepGoing)
{
    var key = Console.ReadKey();
    if (key.Key == ConsoleKey.Enter)
    {
        keepGoing = false;
        transformer.Complete();
        Console.WriteLine("waiting for the queue to flush");
        transformer.Completion.Wait();
        slowDisplay.Complete();
        slowDisplay.Completion.Wait();
        Console.WriteLine("press any key");
        Console.ReadKey();
        break;
    }
    transformer.Post(key.KeyChar);
}
```

7. Run the program. When the console window appears, just randomly press characters, and when you are done hit *Enter*. You should see an output similar to the following. Note how the encoded strings appear in batches up to four, though this may be one or two if you have a CPU with less than four cores.

file:///c:/users/richard/documents/visual studio 11/Projects/DataFlow/DataFlow/bin/Debug/DataFl...

```
lhjsdgfllTA==
SA==
Sg==
Uw==
LKJHGRA==
Rw==
Rg==
TA==
waiting for the queue to flush
TA==
TA==
Sw==
Sg==
SA==
Rw==
press any key
```

How it works...

So what just happened here?

Firstly, you defined two actors. The first being the `ActionBlock` object that takes a string and displays it on screen and a second, the `TransformBlock`, that takes a character as input and returns an encoded string as output. You then linked the `TransformBlock` object to the `ActionBlock` object to create the pipeline for the data to flow through.

Then you took data that was streaming to you (the console key presses) and passed each key press to the pipeline as soon as it arrived. This continued until the user hit *Enter* at which point the `Complete()` method is used to tell the actors that they should expect no more data. Once the queues flush, the user is prompted to hit a key to close the program.

If you fail to flush the queues you will lose the data that is still in them when the program completes. I'm not sure about you, but I find that losing data tends to upset people at times and I prefer not having those "please explain" conversations with people.

Now when you ran the program the `TransformBlock` object did its work very quickly and passed its output to the `ActionBlock`. The interesting thing to note is that even though the data was queuing up to be processed by the `ActionBlock` object, the amount of code you had to write to do that was zero! The TPL Dataflow library takes care of all the difficult plumbing code, thread management, and the communication of data between actors, as well as determining how many actors it can run at once.

There's more...

You may also be wondering what happens in less straightforward scenarios, such as when you want to conditionally pass data or messages to the next actor. Fortunately, the TPL Dataflow Library is quite powerful and you've only scratched the surface in this recipe. For example, the `LinkTo()` method has a predicate parameter that you can use to filter the messages and decide which actors should do what.

You could also batch up data for processing in the later steps by adding data to a buffer using the `BufferBlock` object and only passing buffered data to subsequent pipeline steps when the buffer is full. There are lot of possibilities! Feel free to go and explore what the library has to offer!

The eagle eyed amongst you may also have noticed that the lambda function used by the `ActionBlock` object featured the `async` keyword. This was done so that the action block doesn't itself block execution of the program when performing the long-running task and prevent any more input from being processed.

See also

- ▶ The *Making your code asynchronous* recipe
- ▶ The *Debugging parallel code* recipe in *Chapter 5, Debugging Your .NET Application*

7
Unwrapping C++ Development

In this chapter, we will cover:

- ► Using XAML with C++
- ► Unit testing C++ applications
- ► Analyzing your C++ code
- ► Working with DirectX in Visual Studio 2012
- ► Creating a shader using DGSL
- ► Creating and displaying a 3D model
- ► Using the Visual Studio Graphics Debugger

Introduction

C++ as a language has been declining in use over recent years and becoming more of a specialist language, to the point where it is now commonly seen as the language for writing operating systems, device drivers, games engines, and those rare applications when speed is of the essence.

This decline hasn't been helped by the slow pace of improvements in the C++ language and the volume of code needed when compared to more modern languages. However the introduction of Windows 8 and Visual Studio 2012 sees a chance for the decline to stop. Microsoft has recognized that C++ developers are still a viable and valuable part of the developer ecosystem and that it's about time they got some love. C++ developers will be pleased with the support for C++ 11; the inclusion of reference counting smart pointers alone will make memory management much simpler. They will also be pleased with the tooling improvements Visual Studio 2012 offers and this is what we'll be looking at in the recipes in this chapter.

So without any further ado, let's get to it.

Using XAML with C++

User interface development with C++ has always been, how shall we say it, a less than optimal experience. When Visual Basic first appeared all those years ago developers flocked to it because building a user interface in it was so much more productive than building the equivalent UI using C++ at the time, and C++ has never really caught up since.

Over recent years, with Microsoft's move away from WinForms, and the rise of declarative interface design with XAML, building a flexible yet powerful user interface has never been easier and the functionality offered by XAML based UI technologies is impressive, with data binding in particular being a genuine productivity improver.

Meanwhile, C++ developers have been left further and further behind, with the only interface development using C++ largely being the domain of games studios and the teams within Microsoft building products and platforms.

In Visual Studio 2012, the power and flexibility of XAML based user interface design is now available for C++ developers, making C++ a legitimate choice for business applications.

> C++ and XAML can only be used to create WinRT applications. You cannot use them to create traditional desktop applications.

It's not just business applications that benefit though. Developers of DirectX applications can use XAML to render interface elements and composite them with the rest of the DirectX application. For game developers this might be things like application menus, score displays, and so on. Alternatively, you can have XAML based applications with islands of DirectX in them, allowing developers of applications with a need for 3D imaging such as medical or geospatial systems to mix and match DirectX and XAML as required.

The choice and flexibility is up to you. For this recipe you'll create a simple XAML based interface with data binding to see how it all fits together.

Getting ready

Ensure you are booted into a Windows 8 machine. Windows Store app development is not supported on prior versions of Windows.

Start Visual Studio 2012 and you're ready to go.

How to do it...

Create the app by following these steps:

1. Create a new **Visual C++ | Windows Store | Blank App (XAML)** project and give it the name `CppDataBinding`.

2. Open the `MainPage.xaml` file and add the following code inside the `<Grid>` element:

```xml
<Border BorderBrush="LightBlue" BorderThickness="4" CornerRadius="20" Margin="5">
    <StackPanel Margin="5">
        <TextBlock Text="Red level:" Margin="5" />
        <Slider x:Name="redLevelSlider" Minimum="0"
                Maximum="255" Value="{Binding Path=RedValue, Mode=TwoWay}"
                Margin="5" Width="255" HorizontalAlignment="Left"/>
        <TextBlock Text="Numeric value:" Margin="5"/>
        <TextBox x:Name="tbValueConverterDataBound"
                 Text="{Binding Path=RedValue, Mode=TwoWay}"
                 Margin="5" Width="150" HorizontalAlignment="Left"/>
    </StackPanel>
</Border>
```

3. For the data binding to work you will need an object to bind to. Add a new header file to your project and call it `MyColor.h`. As a note, hold off on compiling the code until you get to step 9; compiling before then will result in compiler errors.

4. Enter the following code as the contents of the `MyColor.h` source file:

```cpp
#pragma once
#include "pch.h"

using namespace Platform;
using namespace Windows::UI::Xaml::Data;

namespace CppDataBinding
{
    [Bindable]
    public ref class MyColor sealed : INotifyPropertyChanged
    {
    public:
        MyColor(void);
        ~MyColor(void);

        virtual event PropertyChangedEventHandler^ PropertyChanged;
        property String^ RedValue
        {
            String^ get() {return _redValue;}
            void set(String^ value)
            {
                _redValue = value;
                RaisePropertyChanged("RedValue");
            }
        }

    protected:
        void RaisePropertyChanged(String^ name);

    private:
        String^ _redValue;
    };
}
```

5. Add a new C++ file named `MyColor.cpp` and enter the following code as its content:

```cpp
#include "pch.h"
#include "MyColor.h"

using namespace CppDataBinding;
using namespace Windows::UI::Xaml::Data;

MyColor::MyColor(void) {}
MyColor::~MyColor(void) {}

void MyColor::RaisePropertyChanged(String^ name)
{
    PropertyChanged(this, ref new PropertyChangedEventArgs(name));
}
```

6. Now go to `MainPage.xaml.h` and add `MyColor.h` to the `#include` list.

7. In the public members of the `MainPage` class add the following highlighted line of code:

```cpp
public:
    MainPage();
    property MyColor^ _myColor;
```

8. Navigate to the code behind for the `MainPage` class (that is, the `MainPage.xaml.cpp` file) and add the following highlighted lines of code to the constructor:

```cpp
MainPage::MainPage()
{
    InitializeComponent();
    _myColor = ref new MyColor();
    this->DataContext = _myColor;
}
```

9. Compile and run the application. You should see a screen similar to the following screenshot appear. As you enter values in the text field or move the slider, the two fields should remain in sync, as shown in the following screenshot:

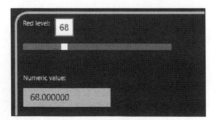

How it works...

The C++ code you have been writing is **C++/CX**; an extension of the normal C++. You can still use straight C++ if you prefer but it will mean dealing with the IInspectable interface and writing more COM code than would otherwise be the case.

The ref keyword you used for creating an instance of the MyColor class tells the compiler that you are using a Windows runtime object. The carat (^) symbol on variable declarations is a reference counting **smart pointer** to a Windows runtime object. It is similar to a normal pointer but performs reference counting and automatic cleanup of resources when the last reference is cleared.

Data binding in C++ kicks into action when you put the [Bindable] attribute on a class. When the compiler sees this it will automatically generate code in a file called xamltypeinfo.g.cpp that implements the appropriate binding behaviors for interacting with the XAML markup.

In your code you implemented the INotifyPropertyChanged interface. This was done so that you could use the two-way binding between the data class and the UI elements on screen. The implementation of the interface should look familiar to anyone who has worked with INotifyPropertyChanged in either WPF or Silverlight before.

There's more...

If you were compiling the code after each step in the recipe you may have seen a few compiler errors, some of which might have not made much sense.

If you compiled the application after step 5 you may have seen a number of errors in XamlTypeInfo.g.cpp.

This occurs because of the way the compiler handles the [Bindable] attribute and the generation of the code. The generated code only includes the .h files from the XAML pages in the application, yet it includes generated code for any types that are bindable. This means that if you have a bindable type but no references to it in any of the .xaml.h files, you will have undeclared identifier errors as shown in the following screenshot:

Adding the #include statement for the bindable class' header file as you did in step 6 fixes this compiler error.

Unit testing C++ applications

We saw the *Unit testing .NET application recipe* in *Chapter 4, .NET Framework 4.5 Development*, C++ developers were not forgotten and Visual Studio 2012 includes support for **cppUnit** for unit testing your applications.

Just to help with the confusion, C++ developers can choose from two types of unit test projects—the **Native Unit Test** project and the **Unit Test Library (Windows Store apps)** project. The first applies exclusively to desktop C++ development, while the second applies exclusively to Windows Store apps.

In this recipe we'll create a simple piece of code and add some unit tests to it.

Getting ready

Simply start Visual Studio 2012 and you're ready to go. You can do this in any version of Windows since you're going to be creating a Native Unit Test.

How to do it...

To unit test your code, follow these steps:

1. Create a new C++ **Test | Native Unit Test** project application using the default name.

2. In **Solution Explorer** right-click on the project and select **Class Wizard** from the menu to create a new class.

3. Click on the **Add Class** button in the dialog to add a new class to the project. Use the class name BankVault and click on **Finish**.

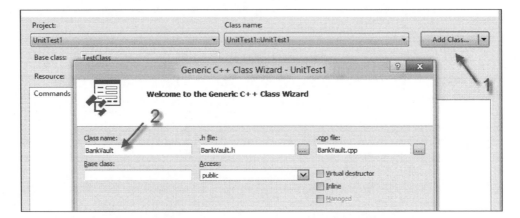

4. The **Class Wizard** will update its context to the newly-added BankVault class. Click on the **Methods** tab and then click on the **Add Method** button within that tab.

5. In the **Add Member Function Wizard** set **Function name** to **AddFunds** and add a parameter named amount of type int (yes, our wonderful bank vault only accepts whole units of currency). Don't forget to click on **Add** to add the parameter!

6. Click on **Finish** in the **Add Member Function Wizard** and then click on **OK** in the **Class Wizard**.

7. Open the `Source Files\unittest1.cpp` file from **Solution Explorer** and at the top of the file add an `#include` statement for `BankVault.h`.

8. Update the body of `TestMethod1` as follows:

```
TEST_METHOD(TestMethod1)
{
    auto vault = new BankVault();
    auto totalFunds = vault->AddFunds(100);
    Assert::AreEqual(100,totalFunds);
}
```

9. From the Visual Studio menu select **Test | Run | All Tests**.

10. The code will compile. **Test Explorer** will then appear and show the results of running the test.

11. From the menu, select **Test | Test Settings | Run Tests After Build** so that the unit tests will run automatically each time the solution is built.

12. Navigate back to the `BankVault.cpp` file and update the code as follows:

```
int total = 0;

int BankVault::AddFunds(int amount)
{
    total += amount;
    return total;
}
```

13. Build the solution and wait a few moments. As soon as the build completes, **Test Explorer** should refresh and show the results of the unit test. Assuming you made the correct changes, the code should now look like the following screenshot:

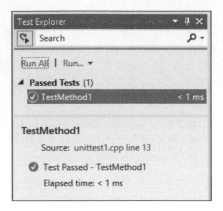

14. Time to add a few new methods. In `BankVault.h` add the following two highlighted lines of code:

```
class BankVault
{
public:
    BankVault(void);
    ~BankVault(void);
    int AddFunds(int amount);
    void StageHeist();
    int CurrentFunds();
};
```

15. In `BankVault.cpp` add the implementation for these two methods as follows:

```
void BankVault::StageHeist()
{
    total = 0;
}

int BankVault::CurrentFunds()
{
    return total;
}
```

16. Now add a test for this code in `unittest1.cpp` by adding the following code:

```
TEST_METHOD(RobTheBank)
{
    auto vault = new BankVault();
    auto totalFunds = vault->AddFunds(200);
    Assert::AreEqual(200,totalFunds);
    vault->StageHeist();
    totalFunds = vault->CurrentFunds();
    Assert::AreEqual(0,totalFunds);
}
```

17. Compile the solution and wait for **Test Explorer** to rerun the tests. You should now see one failing test result and one passing result.

18. There's a small mistake in your code, and clicking on the first line of the stack trace in the error detail should help you isolate the problem (the initial funds aren't as expected). Start to fix the problem by navigating to `BankVault.h` and adding a `private int` variable named `total`.

19. In `BankVault.cpp`, remove the `int total = 0;` declaration and change the class constructor to initialize `total` to `zero`.

20. Compile the code one last time. The tests will be rerun and **Test Explorer** will show all tests working as expected.

How it works...

The test project you created has a reference to the cppUnit test framework already included, as well as the necessary header files to define the various `Assert` methods available and the macros for creating the test methods.

You could build all of this up by hand but there's really no need to when the project template has defined it for you up front.

There are a few slight differences when creating a Unit Test Library project for a Windows Store app. You will be referencing the WinRT libraries instead of normal libraries, you will be using the C++/CX extensions, and you can only add references to other WinRT based libraries.

There's more...

The option to run unit tests with code coverage is available from **Test Explorer**, however for Windows Store app Unit Test Library projects you will get no results as the diagnostic data adapters are not supported for unit tests of Windows Store app libraries.

Coverage information is only supported for **Native Unit Test** projects, and coverage analysis will be displayed in the **Code Coverage Results** window.

Running a unit test in debug mode

In the .NET languages you can right-click inside a test method in the code window and select the option to run and debug a unit test. This isn't available for C++ unit tests.

To debug unit tests you must select them from **Test Explorer** and either right-click on them and choose the **Debug Selected Tests** context menu option or you must select **Test | Debug | Selected Tests** from the Visual Studio menu.

See also

▸ The *Unit testing .NET applications* recipe in *Chapter 4, .NET Framework 4.5 Development*

Analyzing your C++ code

Static analysis of C++ code is a feature offered by Visual Studio 2010 and Visual Studio 2012 continues to build on that feature by making static analysis easier to perform, problems easier to locate, and helps expand the available rules allowing you to catch a wider range of problems earlier.

Getting ready

Start Visual Studio 2012 and create a new C++ **Empty Project**, giving it a name could take this to the previous line.

How to do it...

Perform the following steps:

1. Right-click on the project and select **Properties**.

2. In **Configuration Properties | General** change **Configuration Type** to **Static Library (.lib)** and click on **OK**.

3. Add a new **Header File** to the project and name it `AnalyzeThis.h`.

4. Enter the following code in the body of the header file:

```
class AnalyzeThis{
public:
    int LookHere(int param);
};
```

5. Add a new **C++ File** to the project and name it `AnalyzeThis.cpp`.

6. Enter the following code as the body of the code file:

```cpp
#include "AnalyzeThis.h"

int AnalyzeThis::LookHere(int param)
{
    int x;
    int y;
    if (param > 0) x = param;
    if (param < 0) y = param;
    return x + y;
}
```

7. Compile the project. There should be no errors or warnings showing.

8. Right-click on the project and select **Properties** again. Select the **Code Analysis** group and ensure the rule selected is **Microsoft Native Recommended Rules**. Click on **OK** to close the window.

9. From the **Analyze** menu select **Run Code Analysis on Solution**.

10. The **Code Analysis** tool window will be displayed and it will show a single warning about the use of uninitialized memory, as shown in the following screenshot:

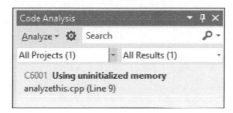

11. Click on the entry to expand it. The reasons for the analysis warning will be shown and the code where the warning occurs will be highlighted in the document window.

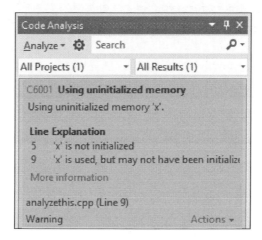

12. Change the code so that both x and y are initialized correctly with zero values.

13. Rerun the analysis. No messages should be displayed.

How it works...

There are two rule sets provided for native code in Visual Studio 2012.

The **Microsoft Native Minimum Rules** rule set contains rules for basic correctness such as potential security holes and application crashes (invalid memory access, buffer overruns, and so on).

The **Microsoft Native Recommended Rules** rule set is a superset of the minimum rules and provides a more in-depth set of rules to evaluate and, with Visual Studio 2012, this includes new rule checks for problems such as lock problems, race conditions, and other concurrency related issues.

To get an understanding of what rules each rule set uses, go to the project properties and select the **Code Analysis** settings. Clicking on the **Open** button will display the rules enabled for the rule set. In order to see all available rules, click on the red down arrow in the toolbar.

Working with DirectX in Visual Studio 2012

C++ and DirectX are being promoted by Microsoft as the primary way to build high performance games in Windows 8 with XNA left out in the cold. XNA developers can still use XNA in Windows 8 but only for desktop applications, not for creating Windows Store apps.

As a DirectX developer you will be pleased there is no longer a separate DirectX download required for Windows 8. The DirectX SDK is now incorporated into the Windows SDK, and the DirectX 11.1 runtime is built into the Windows 8 operating system. For older versions of Windows, the current requirement to download a separate SDK and runtime remains in place.

If you have used previous versions of DirectX and C++ then Visual Studio 2012 will feel somewhat different as you will be using C++/CX and many of the DirectX calls have differences in them, not only due to the use of `ref` pointers but also in the way displays are referenced and the restrictions placed on you by the Windows Store app sandbox. It will likely require some tweaking to the approaches you may have used in the past.

For this recipe, we'll use the default application template to display a rotating cube on screen and then alter the code to stop and start the rotation when we touch the screen, click the mouse, or press a key.

Getting ready

Start Visual Studio 2012 in Windows 8 and you're ready to go.

How to do it...

Create the app by following these steps:

1. Create a new **Visual C++ | Windows Store | Direct3D App** project and name it `RotatingCube`.

2. The default project template includes all the code to display a cube, apply shaders to it, and then rotate it. Before you go any further, ensure that the application works, by compiling and running it. You should see a screen similar to the following screenshot:

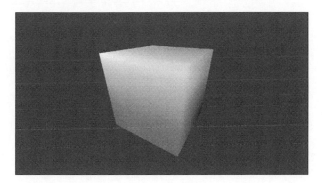

3. Stop the application by pressing *Alt+F4* and then switch back to Visual Studio. In `RotatingCube.h` add the following code block to the `protected` event handler declarations:

```
void OnPointerReleased(Windows::UI::Core::CoreWindow^ sender,
        Windows::UI::Core::PointerEventArgs^ args);
void OnKeyDown(Windows::UI::Core::CoreWindow^ sender,
        Windows::UI::Core::KeyEventArgs^ args);
```

4. To the `private` variables in the header file, add `bool m_isRotating;`.

5. In `RotatingCube.cpp`, locate the `RotatingCube::SetWindow` method and add the following highlighted code to register the event handlers for the user input events and to set the `m_isRotating` flag:

```
// Start recieving touch/mouse events and keyboard events
window->PointerReleased +=
        ref new TypedEventHandler<CoreWindow^, PointerEventArgs^>
        (this,&RotatingCube::OnPointerReleased);
window->KeyDown +=
        ref new TypedEventHandler<CoreWindow^, KeyEventArgs^>
        (this,&RotatingCube::OnKeyDown);
m_isRotating = true;

m_renderer->Initialize(CoreWindow::GetForCurrentThread());
```

6. Now add the code for the event handlers. The handlers simply toggle the `m_isRotating` flag to indicate whether to rotate the cube or not.

```
void RotatingCube::OnPointerReleased
        (Windows::UI::Core::CoreWindow^ sender,
        Windows::UI::Core::PointerEventArgs^ args)
{
        m_isRotating = !m_isRotating;
}
void RotatingCube::OnKeyDown
        (Windows::UI::Core::CoreWindow^ sender,
        Windows::UI::Core::KeyEventArgs^ args)
{
        m_isRotating = !m_isRotating;
}
```

7. Locate the `RotatingCube::Run()` method and wrap the `m_renderer->Update` call in an `if` statement that checks the `m_isRotating` flag as shown in the following screenshot:

```
if (m_isRotating)
{
    m_renderer->Update(timer->Total, timer->Delta);
}
```

8. Run the application and check that you can start and stop the rotation by pressing any key, clicking with the mouse, or tapping on the screen.

9. Stop the application when you have finished testing.

10. The colors on the cube are determined by a combination of a vertex shader and a pixel shader. The vertex shader uses the color assigned to each vertex in the cube's definition, in `CubeRenderer::CreateDeviceResources`, and each pixel shader is shaded based on blending the colors of the vertexes nearest to it. Open the `SimplePixelShader.hlsl` file to look at the pixel shader.

11. At the moment the shader simply takes the color passed to it and sets the alpha channel to `1.0f` making it opaque. Alter the shader to remove all trace of red from the cube by changing the body of the `main()` method to the following:

```
float4 main(PixelShaderInput input) : SV_TARGET
{
    float3 removedRed;
    removedRed = float3(0.0f, input.color.g, input.color.b);
    return float4(removedRed,1.0f);
}
```

12. Rebuild and run the application. The cube should now look similar to the following screenshot, with no red color showing:

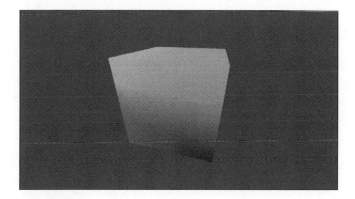

How it works...

The key areas to focus on in this application involve creating the drawing surface and the handling of user input. You saw how user input can be handled via the event listeners and that the `PointerEventArgs` class is used for both touch and mouse-based input.

The bulk of the work to create the rendering surface is encapsulated in the `Direct3DBase` class. It is in here that the call to `D3D11CreateDevice` is made as is the call to `CreateSwapChainForCoreWindow`, which is needed in order to get DirectX up and running correctly.

It is also useful to note that an Application Manifest is included in the project and that the linker has prepopulated references to the required DirectX libraries so that you don't have to remember to add them yourself.

There's more...

The pixel and vertex shaders used in the application are written using HLSL; a C++ style DSL for describing how color should be calculated for each rendered pixel in an object.

When the compiler sees a HLSL file it compiles it into a `.cso` file that you can then use in your application. You can see this in `CubeRenderer::CreateDeviceResourc es()` where the `.cso` files of the two shaders are read into memory and then passed to the DirectX calls to create shader instances. The shaders are then used later in the `CubeRenderer::Render()` method with the vertex shader called before the pixel shader to ensure the cube renders correctly.

Jumpy rotation

When you stop and start the rotation you will notice that the cube jumps in its position and doesn't cleanly resume rotation. If you take a look at the `CubeRenderer::Update` method in `CubeRenderer.cpp` you will see that the algorithm to rotate the cube uses an elapsed time value (`timeTotal`). As an exercise, feel free to alter this code so that the cube resumes its rotation from the point at which it was paused.

Is managed DirectX supported?

With Windows Runtime and the improvements in the way .NET languages interop with COM in Windows 8 you may be wondering if DirectX development using managed languages such as C# is possible. The answer is yes, but not without using third-party libraries. If you are interested in using DirectX in a managed language you may want to keep an eye on open source projects such as SharpDX (`http://code.google.com/p/sharpdx/`). Just keep in mind that this approach is not supported by Microsoft and that DirectX applications written in .NET will run a little slower than native C++ applications. Regardless, applications built using third-party libraries such as SharpDX and others should still be able to pass the verification process and be listed in the store.

See also

▸ The *Creating a Windows Store app* recipe in *Chapter 2, Getting Started with Windows Store Applications*

▸ The *Creating a shader using DGSL* recipe

▸ The *Using the Visual Studio Graphics Debugger* recipe

Creating a shader using DGSL

With Visual Studio 2012, Microsoft has added a new mechanism for building shaders, using a language called **DGSL (Directed Graph Shader Language)**. This language can be used to create very complex shaders that are still easily understandable at a high level and are thus more maintainable than shaders written in pure HLSL.

In this recipe, we'll create a shader that applies a texture to an object and colors it.

Getting ready

Ensure you are running Windows 8 and start Visual Studio 2012.

How to do it...

Create a shader by following these steps:

1. Create a new **Visual C++ | Windows Store | Direct3D App** project and give it the default name.

2. Right-click on the project, select **Add | New Item**, and then choose **Graphics | Visual Shader Graph (.dgsl)**. Leave the name as the default, `Shader.dgsl`, and click on **Add**.

3. The shader will be added to the project and the design surface will be displayed. Open the toolbox to see all the nodes that can be used in your shader. Click on the black background of the design surface to see the properties of the shader.

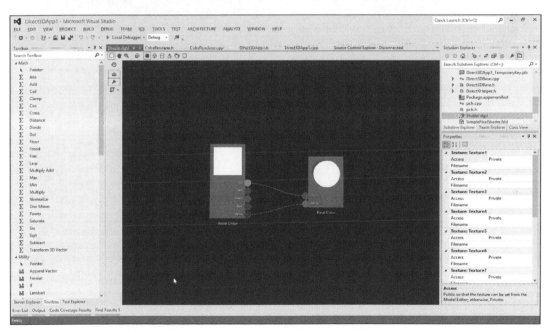

4. From the **Toolbox** window, drag a **Texture Sample** node onto the design surface.

If you have trouble finding the Texture Sample in the toolbox, use the search box at the top of the toolbox to filter the items displayed.

5. In the properties for the **Texture Sample** node you just added, set the **Filename** to the full path of the `Assets\SmallLogo.png` file. You can do this fairly easily by selecting the image file in **Solution Explorer**, copying the **Full Path** from the **Properties** window for the file, and pasting that value into the **Filename** property of the **Texture Sample** node.

6. Drag a **Texture Coordinate** node from the **Toolbox** window onto the design surface.

7. On the side of each of the shader nodes are connectors; the small circles that represent the input and output variables for each node. Drag the **Output** connector of the **Texture Coordinate** node to the **UV** input connector of the **Texture Sample** node to link the two nodes together.

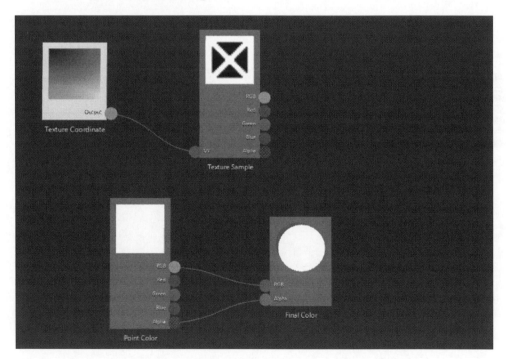

8. Next, you should color the texture based on the color of the point at which it will be applied. To do this, drag a **Multiply** node onto the designer and connect the **RGB** output of both the **Point Color** and **Texture Sample** nodes to the **X** and **Y** inputs of the **Multiply** node.

9. Next, drag the **result** output of the **Multiply** node to the **RGB** input of the **Final Color** node. In doing so, the **RGB** link from the **Point Color** node to the **Final Color** node will be removed as inputs can only have one source.

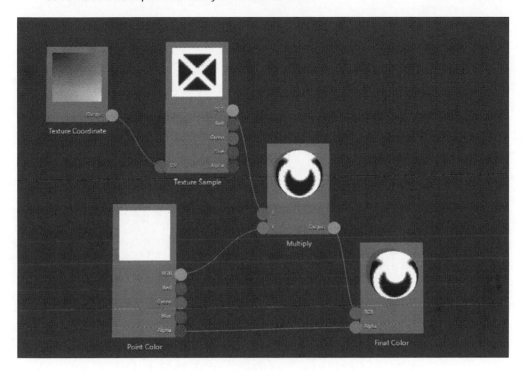

10. In the document toolbar, click on the **Preview with teapot** button. Why a teapot? Because it wouldn't be 3D rendering if there wasn't a teapot involved!

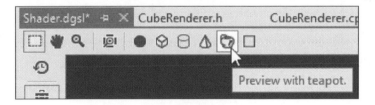

11. In the shader designer, select the **Final Color** node and then hold down *Ctrl* while you move the mouse scroll wheel forward to zoom in on the element until you can zoom no further. You will now see a better 3D representation of what the shader will do to a model.

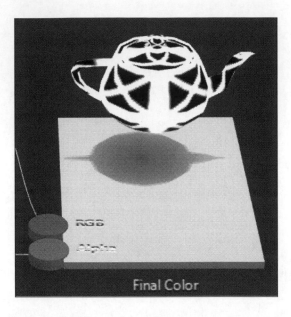

12. Press and hold *Alt* and then click-and-drag on the teapot to rotate it so that you have a better idea of how the texture will be applied to the various surfaces of the teapot.

13. Save the `Shader.dgml` file by pressing *Ctrl+S*.

14. In the designer's left-side toolbar, click on the **Advanced** icon. It will launch an Export command where you can choose to save the shader as HLSL, a compiled pixel shader (`.cso`), or as a C++ header file (`.h`). Select the HLSL file option and save the shader into your `Documents` folder.

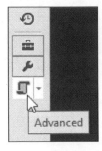

15. From the Visual Studio menu, select **File | Open | File** or press *Ctrl+O* and then open the file you just saved. You can now see the HLSL version of the shader you created.

How it works...

Shaders are effectively a pipeline of instructions to affect the rendering of an object on screen. They can be applied to vertices, pixels, and geometries to produce varying effects. The key to all shaders is to try and do as few operations as possible since the higher the number of nodes in a shader the more computationally expensive they will be and the slower your overall frame rate in the application will be.

In this particular recipe, the shader we built was fairly rudimentary since the intent was to show how one can be built in Visual Studio. For complex shaders such as flame or smoke there are parameter nodes for **Time** and **Normalized Time** that you will want to use, and for geometry shaders you will want to consider using nodes such as **World Position** and **Mask Vector**.

See also

▸ The *Creating and displaying a 3D model* recipe

▸ The *Working with DirectX in Visual Studio 2012* recipe

Creating and displaying a 3D model

In the previous recipe, *Creating a shader using DGSL*, you created a shader for applying a texture to a model. This is great, but without having a model to apply the shader to it's kind of useless. It would be great if there was an easy way to create your own 3D models and Visual Studio provides a mechanism for doing just that. Visual Studio offers a fairly basic 3D modeling tool and, while it's nowhere near as fully featured as Maya or other specialist modeling tools, it does come in the box and it meets the needs of the homebrew developer or those simply wanting to "rough in" some models or tweak some properties of a model supplied by a designer.

Getting ready

This recipe uses the shader from the previous *Creating a shader using DGSL* recipe. So, if you haven't already completed that, go ahead and do so now.

If you have already completed it then go ahead, open up the solution you created and you're ready to get started.

How to do it...

Create a 3D model using the following steps:

1. Right-click on the project and select **Add | New Item**.

2. In the dialog box, choose **Graphics | 3D Scene (.fbx)** and leave the name as Scene. fbx before clicking on **Add**.

3. Visual Studio will open the scene editor where you can create your model. Ensure the **Toolbox** and **Properties** panes are visible, and then add a cylinder to the scene by double-clicking on the **Cylinder** in the **Toolbox** window.

4. Select the cylinder in the designer by clicking on it. In the scene editor toolbar at the left of the design surface click on the scale icon. The cylinder will be overlaid with x, y, and z drag handles (the red, green, and blue boxes) that you can use to resize the object in any single direction and a central drag handle (a white box) for scaling the object evenly in all directions. Resize the cylinder to make it larger by clicking on the central white handle and dragging it to the right.

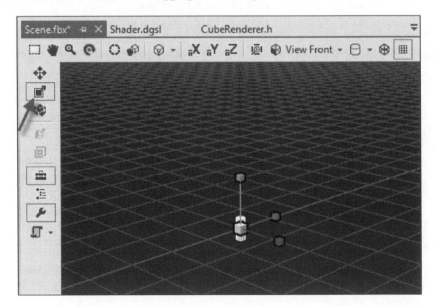

5. In the **Properties** window, locate the **Effect** property.

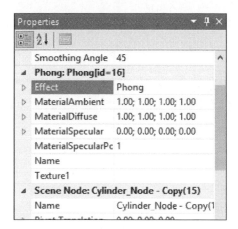

6. Click on the triangle next to the **Effect** property to expand its details and click on the ellipsis [**...**] on the **Filename** property to open the file selection dialog.

7. Browse for the `Shader.dgsl` file you created in the previous recipe and click on **OK**.

8. Change the value of the **Name** property in the **Shader** property group to **MyShader**.

9. Once you've made the shader changes you may notice that the name of the shader property group in the **Properties** window didn't change. Don't panic. It will refresh the next time the **Properties** window is asked to display properties for the cylinder. You can force this by clicking on a file in **Solution Explorer** and then clicking on the cylinder again. You should also see that the scene has been updated to show the effects of the shader on the cylinder.

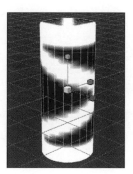

10. A common way of looking at 3D models is to look at the wireframe. To view the scene in wireframe mode click on the wireframe icon on the main toolbar (not the embedded toolbar). It's the last icon in the list, as shown in the following screenshot:

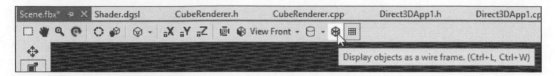

How it works...

At this point you now have a model that is ready to be used. As mentioned in the introduction, the modeling tool is not meant to compete with full featured 3D modeling tools and is instead offered as an entry level modeling toolkit only.

Given that the packaging of models is typically application specific, Visual Studio provides no inbuilt method for packing models into a data file nor a method to load them. The choice of how you package models depends on your application, its performance characteristics, and any of the restrictions you have to work within. Because of the diversity, Visual Studio provides a single, simple method for editing a model and for everything else, it's up to you.

There's more...

There are many more features available in the model viewer than were covered in this recipe. Most of these features are self-explanatory and deal with the basics of moving and rotating objects within the scene, changing selection modes, and changing view modes. Advanced functionality such as merging objects is contained under the **Advanced** menu of the designer's left-side toolbar

See also

▶ The *Creating a shader using DGSL* recipe

Using the Visual Studio Graphics Debugger

One of the hard things to do in DirectX applications is to determine the cause of a visual glitch or bug on the screen and there are many websites featuring screenshots taken by gamers of weird things happening in a game.

Visual Studio 2012 addresses some of the debugging issues for DirectX applications by including in it a new feature called the Graphics Debugger that lets you look at pixel history to determine just how a specific pixel came to be rendered on screen. Let's see how it works.

Getting ready

Simply start Visual Studio 2012 and you're ready to go.

How to do it...

Perform the following steps:

1. Create a new **Visual C++ | Windows Store | Direct3D App** project and leave the default name as it is.

2. The project template includes code to display a spinning cube, so build the application to ensure it compiles.

3. Start the graphics debugger by pressing *Alt+F5* or by choosing **Debug | Graphics | Start Diagnostics** from the Visual Studio menu.

4. When the application starts you should see the debugger HUD displayed in the top-left corner of the application.

5. While the application is running press *Print Screen* a few times to capture some frames from the application. The debugger HUD should update to display **Captured frame** indicating the capture was successful.

6. Stop debugging when you are ready, and in Visual Studio you should see something similar to the following screenshot:

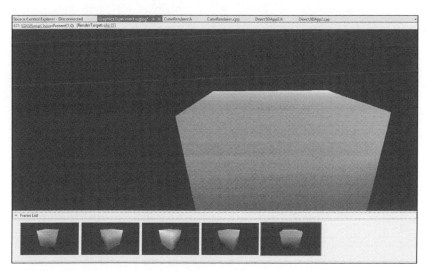

7. Select one of the frames you captured from the **Frame List** window and in the frame view click on one of the pixels in the cube. If you can't see the entire frame you can hold *Ctrl* and drag with the left mouse button to pan around the frame.

8. The Graphics Pixel History window should have appeared when you clicked the pixel. If it isn't showing, in the graphics toolbar click on the **Pixel History** icon (it's the one that looks like a clock going backwards, third from the left).

9. The history of that selected pixel will be shown on the screen.

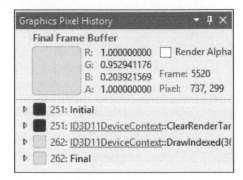

In the previous screenshot, this selected pixel started as blue (the background color) and was eventually rendered as yellow. Your color will likely be different. Click on the expansion arrow for the event when the color changes to expand it.

10. Expand the **Triangle** further to show all of its component details.

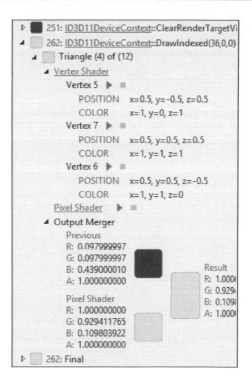

11. Clicking either on the **Vertex Shader** or **Pixel Shader** links will take you to the HLSL source for the shader so you can see the shader calculation.

12. You can examine how the shader values were calculated even after normal debugging has concluded. Click on the **Debug** icon (the play button) for one of the vertices in the vertex shader or for the pixel shader to debug it using the captured values. Step through the shader code until the debugger finishes.

13. From the Visual Studio menu select **Debug | Graphics | Event Call Stack** or click on the **Event Call Stack** button in the Graphics toolbar. The **Event Call Stack** window will be displayed, similar to the following screenshot:

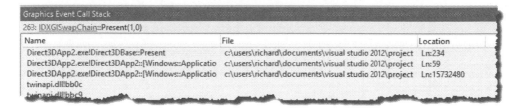

14. This is a normal call stack, so double-click one of the method calls from your application to jump to that line of code.

15. From the Visual Studio menu select **Debug | Graphics | Event List** or click the **Event List** icon on the Graphics toolbar. A list of all DirectX operations that occurred in rendering the frame will be shown.

    Clicking any of the events will show the operation details in the document area allowing you to delve further into what occurred. It will also update the **Event Call Stack** window to show call stack information, when available, and the frame preview window to show what the frame looked like at that specific point in time, which can be very helpful in locating overdraw problems.

How it works...

The Graphics Debugger is the result of the work that was put into the PIX debugging tool that shipped with the DirectX SDK. With it now being built directly into Visual Studio, the user experience is much better for developers.

The level of detail presented by the Graphics Debugger is extensive and should help you track down to the root cause of many of your rendering problems. Of course, fixing them and getting your code right is going to be up to you!

There's more...

One thing that wasn't touched on in the recipe was the rendering pipeline. If you want to look at the way a frame was built up then understanding how the object meshes were used can be very useful.

If you select a DirectX Draw event from the **Events List** and then select **Debug | Graphics | Pipeline Stages** from the menu you will see how the frame was put together. Clicking on one of the stages in the **Graphics Pipeline Stages** window will show you the details of that stage in a document preview tab as shown in the following screenshot:

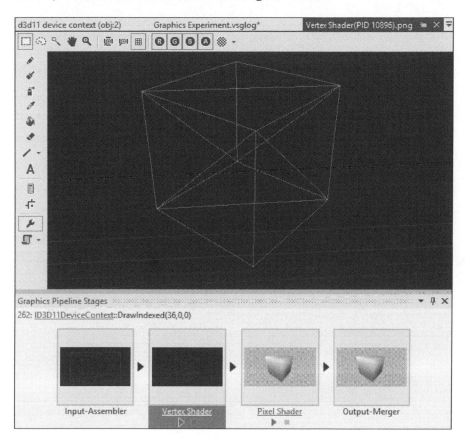

8
Working with Team Foundation Server 2012

In this chapter, we will cover:

- ▶ Managing your work
- ▶ Using local workspaces for source control
- ▶ Storyboarding user requirements
- ▶ Performing code reviews
- ▶ Getting feedback from your users

Introduction

Visual Studio 2012 includes an overhauled Team Explorer client for connecting to Team Foundation Server 2012 (TFS) and the hosted TFS service currently known as TFS Preview.

One of Microsoft's goals with this release of Visual Studio was to have "raving fans". They want users of Visual Studio to be so happy with the experience that they go and tell others about it and how great it is to use. One part of meeting this goal has been to improve the experience developers have when using TFS and, as a result, a number of the main friction and pain points people have had are now smoothed over. In addition a number of new features have also been added to make using TFS more compelling for developers.

The most visible change is in Team Explorer with the transition from a tree view of items to a set of task-based hubs built around the activities that developers need to perform.

The second is the introduction of local workspaces for source control and the decision to make these the default for new workspaces. Local workspaces address the primary grievance developers have with TFS; that source control is managed by the server, not the client, and that the read-only flag is set, making editing of source controlled files outside of Visual Studio difficult.

As for new team-related features, Microsoft has added a lightweight UI prototyping tool, the ability to perform code reviews and an effective way to gather feedback from users on the features you have developed.

The recipes in this chapter will walk you through using these new improvements and features, so let's get started.

Managing your work

If you work in a team then odds are you will have a list of requirements describing what you need to build. Scrum teams use product backlogs, traditional teams use functional specifications, and other teams will have their own variations of these. With TFS this information is stored in the various work item types in the team project.

Regardless of the mechanics used for tracking the work to be done, every developer really just wants the answer to one simple question: "What am I meant to be working on now?".

The new task-based Team Explorer in Visual Studio 2012 makes this question much easier to answer. It also makes it simpler to track what you are doing.

In this recipe, we'll show you how to manage your work using Visual Studio 2012 and TFS.

Getting ready

You will need to have access to a TFS server. It would be best if you use a sandbox project; a project where you can try things and change data without worrying about it affecting your normal work.

The recipe also requires that your team project be based on the Microsoft Visual Studio Scrum 2.0 process template. If your project uses a different process template the work item types may be different from those in the recipe.

Start Visual Studio 2012 and you're ready to go.

How to do it...

Perform the following steps:

1. When you first connect to a TFS server you will need to set up the connection. From *the Visual Studio menu* select **Team | Connect to Team Foundation Server**. Use the **Servers** button in the connection dialog to add a new connection for the TFS server you want to connect to, just like you did in Visual Studio 2010, and then connect to the project collection and the specific team project you wish to use for this recipe.

2. If the **Team Explorer** tool window isn't visible, open it by selecting **View | Team Explorer** from the menu, by pressing *Ctrl+\, Ctrl+M*, or by using the **Quick Launch** tool.

3. When it is open, ensure you are connected to your TFS server by confirming that the **Home** hub is displaying the correct team project name.

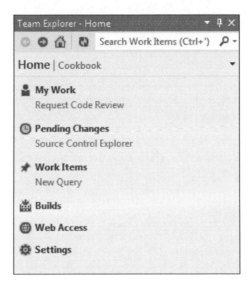

 Your **Home** hub may look slightly different if your team project has a team portal or reporting is enabled.

4. This recipe needs some work for you to track, so start out by creating a new work item. Click on the **Work Items** entry in **Team Explorer** to navigate to the **Work Items** hub. Alternatively, select the **Work Items** hub from the hub list at the top of **Team Explorer,** as shown in the following screenshot:

5. Click on the **New Work Item** drop down from the **Work Items** hub and select **Product Backlog Item** from the list.

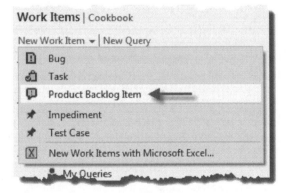

6. A new **Work Item** form will be displayed in the Visual Studio document area. Enter a title of your choice and set the **Assigned To** user to yourself. You can set the value of any of the other fields as you wish and when you are ready click on the **Save Work Item** button in the form's toolbar or press *Ctrl+S* to save the work item.

7. Right-click on the background of the **Product Backlog Item** form (that is, right-click in the white space) and select the **New Linked Work Item** option.

8. In **Work Item Type,** select **Task** from the list and enter a **Title** for the item before clicking on **OK**.

9. The linked work item will have automatically set you to be the **Assigned To** person so just hit *Ctrl + S* to save the work item, or click on the **Save Work Item** button.

10. In **Team Explorer,** switch to the **My Work** hub by using the hub selection drop down. The hub will then display all the work you currently have to do, including any work items assigned to you.

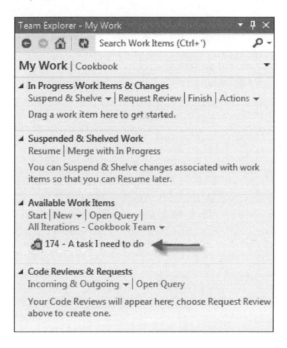

11. To commence work on the task, simply select it and click on **Start** or drag it up to the **In Progress Work Items & Changes** section of the hub.

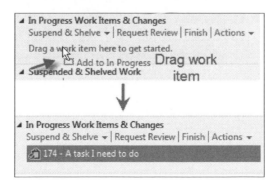

12. Behind the scenes the task will be moved to the **In Progress** state and will also be automatically associated with any source control check-ins that occur. Pretend you did some useful work on the item, then complete it by clicking on the **Finish** link in **Team Explorer** followed by **Yes** in the confirmation dialog that appears. If only all your tasks were so simple to do!

13. To confirm that the work item is actually complete, search for it using the **Work Item Search** field. Enter a few words from the work item title, as shown in the following screenshot:

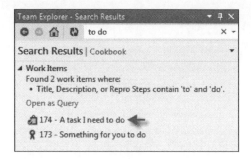

14. Double-click on the task from the **Search Results** to open it and confirm that the **State** of the work item is now **Done**.

How it works...

The work items for both the **In Progress Work Items & Changes** and the **Available Work Items** sections of the **My Work** hub are sourced from a work item query that selects work items of the "task" category, which have a state of **To Do** or **In Progress**. You can check the details of the query by selecting the **Open Query** link in the **My Work** hub and then clicking on the **Edit Query** button in the query results to see the specifics of the query definition. The task category doesn't have to be limited to just the **Task** work item type, but can also incorporate any custom work item types you include in the task category.

If you double-click on a work item in **Team Explorer** that isn't already opened, it is opened by default in the preview pane in Visual Studio to prevent window clutter.

There's more...

The **My Work** hub encourages you to only have one logical task in progress at a time. This can help you limit the amount of work in progress you have and push you towards finishing a task completely before starting the next one. Doing one thing at a time is generally a more productive approach to getting things done than having a lot of different items in progress at once, never finishing them, and spending all your time context switching between them. If you want to improve your personal productivity and work smarter, not harder, then this is a good practice to follow.

On the flip side, if you only work on one thing at a time then what happens when you have to pause what you are doing and deal with an emergency issue?

If you have used previous versions of TFS you may be familiar with the concept of shelving and unshelving code. Shelving takes a copy of the changes you have made, stores them on the server, and then optionally resets your local workspace. Unshelving is just the reverse of that.

In previous versions of Visual Studio, shelving is generally used to either pause work so an urgent task can be attended to, or as a means of sending code to a colleague for a code review. Shelvesets could also be associated with work items so that the context of the task being worked on was retained when the shelveset was created, but as the user experience wasn't great, most people didn't bother tracking the information.

With Visual Studio 2012 and TFS 2012, the two main shelving activities have been streamlined and made explicit. Pausing work is now simply a matter of clicking on the **Suspend & Shelve** link in the **My Work** hub. This automatically shelves your current changes, the work items that were in progress, and the current state of your Visual Studio windows when you hit the button. It then resets your workspace, clears the work items that were in progress, and puts you back in a state ready to start another work item.

The work that you had going is then visible in the **Suspended & Shelved Work** area as shown in the following screenshot:

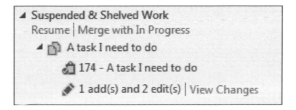

See also

- ▶ The *Using local workspaces for source control* recipe
- ▶ The *Performing code reviews* recipe

Using local workspaces for source control

By far the biggest gripe that most people have with previous versions of TFS is the source control management system and the server-based workspace approach. With this approach the server keeps track of what files it thinks you have on your development machine, and all check-in and check-out operations require communication with the server.

It makes offline work very difficult, and if ever there are changes on your development machine that the server isn't aware of, you can have problems during check-ins and "get latest" operations. To prevent this from happening, TFS sets the read-only flag on all files that are under source control, but this only frustrates developers more since they can't easily edit files unless they use a tool that knows how to communicate with TFS.

There are valid reasons for a server-side workspace approach related to managing extremely large source repositories (think multiple gigabytes of source) and you can still use server-side workspaces if you wish, but for the overwhelmingly large majority of developers, it is an optimization and tax on development practices that simply isn't needed.

TFS 2012 sees the arrival of a Subversion style approach to source control with the introduction of local workspaces.

With local workspaces, the TFS server is still the source of truth for source control and is the only place to which check-ins can occur. However, the decision over which files have been changed now occurs on your development machine, not the TFS server. Further, Visual Studio no longer needs to ask the TFS server if it can open a file for editing or not. Also, you can use any program you want to edit files because the read-only flag is no longer applied to files. This change also improves the offline editing scenario and you no longer need to mess around with the "go offline" and "go online" operations that were required with previous TFS versions.

In this recipe, we'll make some changes to the source code so that you can see how the new approach to source control works.

Getting ready

You will need to have access to a TFS server in order to follow this recipe. It would be best if you also had a sandbox team project; a project where you can try things and change data without worrying about it affecting your normal work.

Start Visual Studio 2012, connect to your team project and you're ready to go.

How to do it...

Perform the following steps:

1. Create a new Visual Basic .NET class library using the default name. Ensure that the **Add to source control** flag is turned on.

2. If you choose a local path for your project that is not already mapped to a folder in source control, you will be prompted for a location in TFS where it should be stored. Select a folder in your source control tree in which to store the project and click on **OK**.

3. In **Team Explorer,** navigate to the **Pending Changes** hub. The files that will be added to source control are shown in the **Included Changes** section.

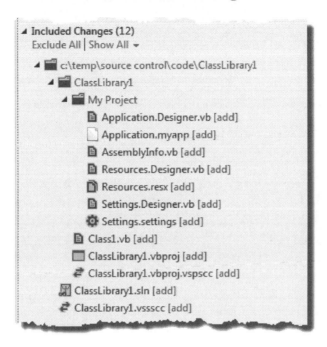

4. Enter a check-in **Comment** to describe what you are doing and then click on **Check In** to submit the changes to TFS. If you are asked to confirm your check-in, click on **Yes**.

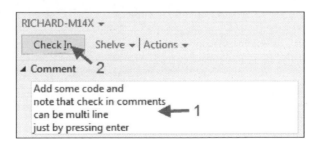

5. The files will be checked-in and a confirmation of the changes will be displayed in **Team Explorer**. If you wish to look at the contents of the changeset you can click on the changeset number displayed in the notification.

6. In **Solution Explorer,** right-click on the class library project and select **Open Folder** in **Windows Explorer**.

7. Right-click on `Class1.vb` and open the file with Notepad.

8. Add some comments to the body of the class, save your changes, and then close Notepad.

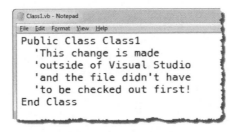

9. Switch back to Visual Studio and, if prompted to reload any files, select **Yes to All**.

10. In **Solution Explorer** you should now see that `Class1.vb` has been modified (it will have a tick next to it). Navigate to **Team Explorer** and within that, go to the **Pending Changes** hub. You should now see that `Class1.vb` is listed as a pending change.

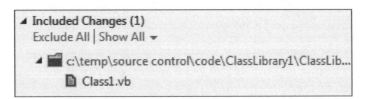

11. Switch back to Windows Explorer and make a copy of `Class1.vb`. Edit the file in Notepad and change the class name to `Class2`. Alter the comments in the body of the class to differentiate it further from the original before saving it and closing Notepad.

Switch back to Visual Studio, and navigate to the **Team Explorer | Pending Changes** hub. The new file you just added won't be listed as an included change, but it has been detected as a change. Since it's not part of the solution, you will only see it by looking at the **Excluded Changes** section and clicking on the **Detected changes** link.

Instead of including the file into source control directly, you'll want to add it to the solution properly. To do so, navigate to **Solution Explorer** and click on the **Show All Files** button on the toolbar.

12. Right-click on `Class 1 - Copy.vb` and click on **Include in Project**.

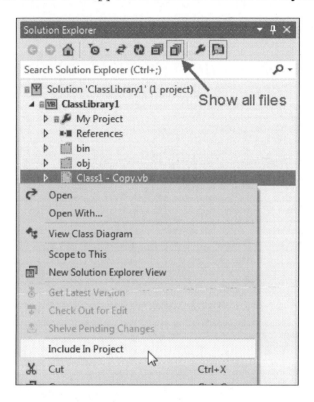

13. Navigate to **Team Explorer** and the **Pending Changes** hub again and confirm that the file is now included as a pending change as shown in the following screenshot. Add a check-in **Comment** and then **Check In** the changes.

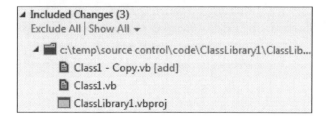

14. A file name of `Class1 - Copy.vb` is embarrassingly bad. You could rename the file in **Solution Explorer** to `Class2.vb` but that would be too easy! Instead switch to Windows Explorer and perform the rename there.

15. Switch back to Visual Studio and navigate to the **Pending Changes** hub in **Team Explorer**. The rename isn't detected automatically since it wasn't made in Visual Studio, however you may notice that there are two changes in the **Detected Changes** section.

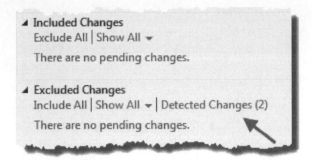

16. Click on the **Detected Changes** link and you will see that the rename is detected as a **delete** of the old filename and an **add** of the new filename. You can let Visual Studio know that this change is actually a rename by selecting both changes in the add/delete pair, right-clicking one and choosing the **Promote as Rename** option. When you have done this click on the **Cancel** button to close the window.

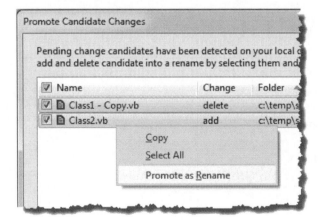

17. Not only is the rename now listed in the **Included Changes** section, but the solution file has also been updated to reflect the change and is also included as a pending change. Very cool! The **Pending Changes** hub should now look like the following screenshot:

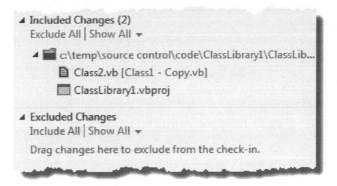

18. Check-in your changes when you are ready.

How it works...

When using a local workspace, Visual Studio creates a hidden local folder named $tf and stores within it zipped copies of the workspace version of your source files. Visual Studio detects changes by comparing the contents of your local files and folders to the contents of the $tf folder and adds any differences as pending changes.

 It might be an obvious warning, but don't delete the $tf folder or any of its contents, not even if you are short on disk space. Doing so will cause problems.

You might have noticed that at no time during the recipe did you have to change the read-only flag on any of the files, nor did you have to check-out any files for edit. In fact the only time Visual Studio communicated with the TFS server was during the check-in process. All other changes were managed and tracked locally.

This should alleviate a lot of pain for people who have been used to older versions of TFS and the way server tracked workspaces operated.

 You cannot check in when offline. Check in operations are still server based and require that you be online and connected to the TFS server.

The detected changes list can grow quite large over time and you may want to ignore certain folders or files (for example, the /obj and /bin folders). You can either create .tfignore files to specify what files and paths to ignore, or in **Team Explorer** you can open the list of detected changes and exclude files either individually, by extension, or by folder path. Doing so will create or alter .tfignore files for you and add them to the pending changes list so that they can be checked-in and shared with all the other developers on the team.

There's more...

Be aware that when using a local workspace, you will no longer have any real visibility on the server over who has checked-out a file. The exception to this is locking files. If you lock a file the server is notified and can report that you have locked it.

Unshelving a shelveset now merges any shelveset changes with your local edits. Hooray! Any conflicts between the shelveset and your local version will cause a merge conflict and you will need to resolve it in the normal manner.

For fans of git (a distributed version control system), Microsoft has recently announced a TFS plugin for git and made it available at `http://gittf.codeplex.com`. You can now have a local git repository that can push/pull from a TFS server. Nice!

See also

► The *Managing your work* recipe

Storyboarding user requirements

To help developers improve communication with their stakeholders, Microsoft has added a tool known as **Storyboarding**. A storyboard is a set of wireframes and mockups that visually describe how an application's user interface should work and the interactions that can occur within that interface.

For Visual Studio 2010 Microsoft pushed Sketch Flow as the tool for UI prototyping. But it is a complex tool with a fairly steep learning curve, especially for people who aren't familiar with XAML. People instead turned to lightweight tools such as Balsamiq because of their ease of use and effectiveness.

Visual Studio 2012's Storyboarding tool is a simple tool much like the other lightweight prototyping tools, with the benefit that it is built directly into PowerPoint, making it not only easy to mock up a user interface, but also to add animations and show UI ideas to a room of people.

In this recipe, you'll create a (very) simple UI prototype with some navigation using the Storyboarding tool.

Getting ready

Open PowerPoint and you're ready to get started.

How to do it...

Create a Storyboard using these steps:

1. In the PowerPoint ribbon, select the **Storyboarding** tab.

2. When you open PowerPoint the default presentation has a single slide that uses the **Title Slide** layout. Using the **Layout** button on the ribbon, change this to the **Blank** layout in order to remove the placeholders from the slide.

3. Click on the **Storyboard Shapes** button in the ribbon to show the **Storyboard Shapes** tool window.

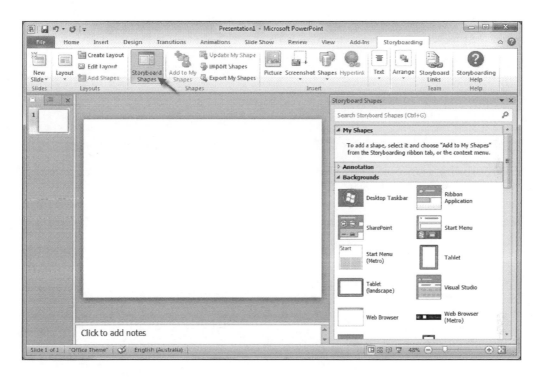

4. In the **Backgrounds** category, double-click on the **Web Browser (Windows 8)** item to add it to the slide. Position it at the bottom of the slide as shown in the following screenshot:

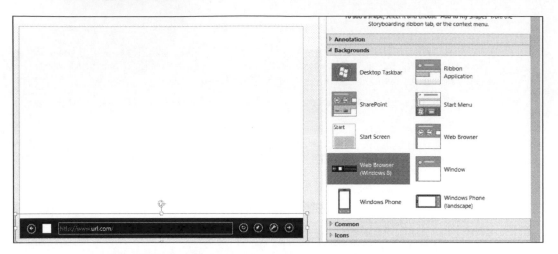

5. In the **Common** category, double-click on the **List** shape to add it to the slide.

6. Now grab the bottom-right drag handle of the shape and change the width and height of the list box as shown in the following screenshot:

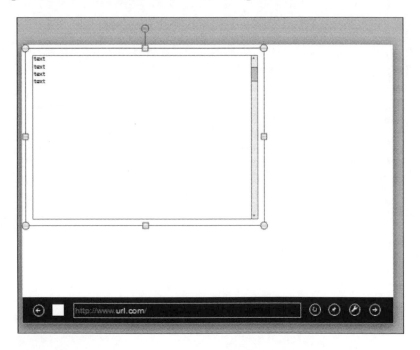

7. Add a new slide to the presentation and then navigate back to the first slide.

8. Select the web browser control at the bottom of slide 1 and then click on the next button within the control so that it is selected.

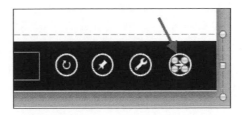

9. Now right-click on the selected shape and choose **Hyperlink** from the context menu.

10. In the dialog box, choose **Place in This Document** from the **Link to** options, select **Next Slide** from the **Select a place in this document** options, and then click on **OK**.

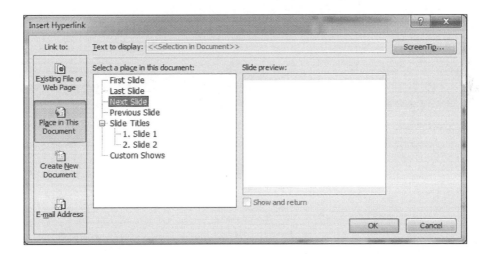

11. Press *F5* to start the presentation.

12. Click on the next button in the address bar to advance to the blank slide. The blank slide represents the next screen/page you might have in your application.

How it works...

Building the layout of an application is simply a matter of placing the appropriate shapes on slides. Anyone who knows how to use PowerPoint should feel right at home doing this. By leveraging that inbuilt functionality you were also able to run a slide show and click elements of your storyboard to simulate navigation.

What you may not have noticed was the automatic resizing applied to the list box's scroll bar when the list box was resized. Normally if you change the size of a PowerPoint shape all the elements of the shape are resized equally. This would mean the scroll bar should have been resized when the list box was made larger, but that would make it look very wrong. To prevent this from happening, the storyboard shapes have metadata in them to specify which elements are resizable and in which directions. For example, the scroll bar wasn't resized for width but it was for height, and the up/down arrows at the ends of the scroll bar remained a single, static size.

There's more...

Some of the shapes include animations in them, such as the **Click** shape. When you add the **Click** shape to your slide you will see the path the shape will travel along when the animation begins. Simply resize and reposition this path as desired and you can easily add simulated interactivity to your prototypes and further improve understanding of how the user interface should behave.

Storyboards make most sense when they are linked to work items and used as design notes, with the new process templates in TFS 2012 specifically catering for this.

In order to link a storyboard to a work item the PowerPoint file needs to be saved to a shared location (that is, a network share). Once that is done you can click on the **Storyboard Links** button in the **Storyboarding** ribbon to begin the process.

In the dialog box, click on the **Link to** button, find the work item you want to attach the storyboard to, and then click on **OK**.

The storyboard will then be linked to the work item(s) as shown in the following screenshot:

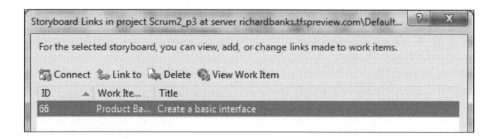

Clicking on the **View Work Item** link will display the selected work item's details and clicking on the **Storyboards** tab of that work item will show the linked storyboard(s).

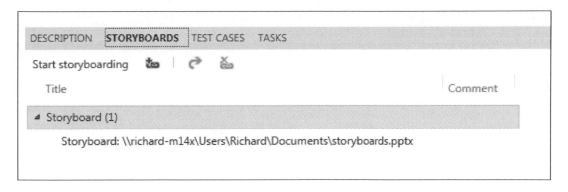

Obviously, if you saved the storyboard to a network location that others can't access, you won't be helping the team very much, so make sure storyboards are saved to shares that the whole team can access, or use your SharePoint project portal (if you have one).

Performing code reviews

When developing in a team, one of the more widely recommended practices for improving code quality and overall consistency is to conduct code reviews.

Visual Studio 2012 combined with TFS 2012 supports the code review process and does so in a very straightforward manner.

In this recipe you'll see just how this works.

Getting ready

You will need to have access to a TFS server in order to follow this recipe. It would be best if you use a sandbox team project, a project where you can try things and change data without worrying about it affecting your normal work.

You will also need to have two accounts you can use; one for the *submitter* of the code review and one for the *reviewer*. If you don't personally have two accounts, that's ok. Just get a colleague to act as your reviewer, it's what you'd need to do in a real project in any case!

Start Visual Studio 2012 and connect to your team project using the submitter's account.

How to do it...

Perform a code review using the following steps:

1. Start a new C# **ASP.NET MVC 4 Web Application** project using the **Internet Application** template and add the solution to source control. See the *Using local workspaces for source control* recipe if you're not sure how to do this.

2. Go to the **Pending Changes** hub in **Team Explorer** and check-in the code.

3. Open the `Controllers\HomeController.cs` file and remove the blank lines from the controller methods, change the contents of the message text, and change the name of the `About` method to `AboutUs`.

4. Open the `Views\Home\Index.cshtml` view and alter the text of the page to something you like. The **Pending Changes** hub should now look like the following screenshot:

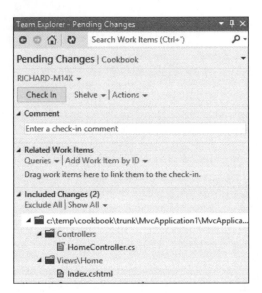

5. Click on the **Actions** drop-down menu and select **Request Review**.

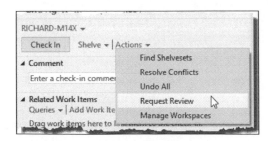

6. In the **New Code Review** pane, enter the name of your reviewer and press *Enter*. The reviewer should be the second user account you are using in this recipe, as mentioned in the *Getting Ready* section. Add a subject for the code review, such as **Check my code please** and then click on **Submit Request**.

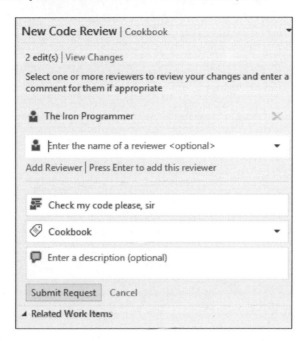

Team Explorer will then switch to the **My Work** hub and show the code review request as an outgoing request.

7. Switch to your reviewer user account, open Visual Studio, and connect to Team Foundation Server.

8. In **Team Explorer,** open the **My Work** hub. You should see a code review request displayed. Note the arrow next to the review indicating it is an incoming request for you to look at.

9. Double-click on the code review to begin the review process. **Team Explorer** will switch to the **Code Review** pane and display the details of the review and information on the files that have been modified.

10. Click on **Accept** in the top section of the **Code Review** window to start the review process and dismiss the accept/reject message.

11. Click on the `HomeController.cs` file in the code review. You will see both the original and modified versions of the file displayed using Visual Studio's new diff viewer.

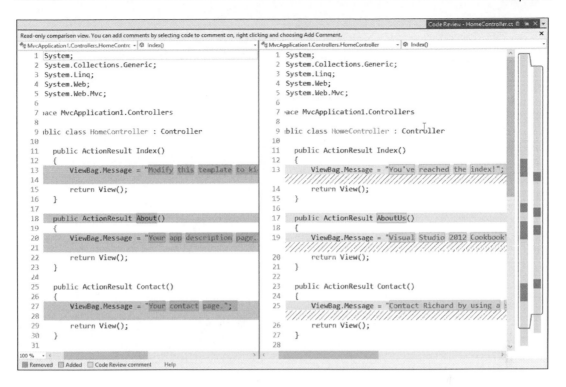

12. Select the entire `AboutUs` method from the right-hand pane, right-click on the selection, and then choose **Add Comment** from the context menu.

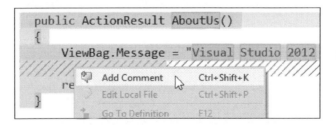

13. The focus switches to the comment box in the **Code Review** pane. Enter a comment, as shown in the following screenshot, and then click on **Save (Ctrl + Enter)**:

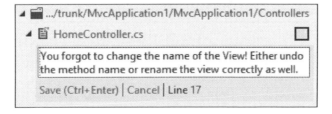

14. Click on the checkbox next to the `HomeController.cs` file in the **Code Review** pane to indicate that there are no further comments to make on that file.

15. Click on the **Add Overall Comment** link and supply a general comment on the code review and then click on **Save (Ctrl + Enter)**.

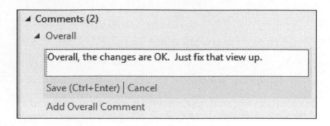

16. Make further comments on the review as you wish and, when you are done, click on the **Send & Finish** link, choosing the **With Comments** option from the drop down that appears.

17. Switch back to the submitter user account. In **Team Explorer,** go to the **My Work** hub and click on the refresh button (assuming you left Visual Studio running). Click on the arrow next to the review request to see the status of the review, and if the review is complete, double-click on it to display the **Code Review** hub.

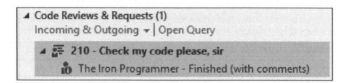

18. Click on the `HomeController.cs` file in the **Code Review** hub and the diff viewer will be displayed, including highlights of where comments have been made by the reviewer.

19. As the submitter you would then take action on the review comments as appropriate, but for the purpose of this recipe, you're going to close the code review. Click on the **Close Review** drop-down link and select **Complete** from the list of options to close the entire code review request.

How it works...

If you noticed, the code review occurred on code that wasn't even checked-in to source control. Behind the scenes, asking for a code review automatically creates a shelveset for the reviewer to look at. Unlike the **Suspend & Shelve** operation, requesting a code review doesn't reset your workspace or clear any of the work items you have marked as in progress.

You can also request reviews for changesets that have already been checked-in and other shelvesets that have been manually created.

See also

▶ The *Managing your work* recipe

▶ The *Using local workspaces for source control* recipe

Getting feedback from your users

When working on a product, one of the most valuable things you can do is get feedback from your users as to whether the software you have built meets their requirements or not, and what their opinions of it are.

Even if you have a process that defines clear acceptance criteria for requirements, and you have a clear definition of what it means to be "done" with a piece of work, you still want feedback from your users to determine whether there are any other points that may have been missed when the requirement was first discussed, or if new ideas have occurred now that they have seen the software running.

A normal feedback process involves telling your users that the software is available and asking them to please go and try it and let you know what they think. The feedback you get can often be patchy, verbally reported, and hard to turn into actionable items for improving the software.

With the new Visual Studio Feedback tool, gathering user feedback becomes a lot simpler to do and fairly straightforward, so let's try it!

Getting ready

Just make sure you have access to a TFS server and team project.

How to do it...

Gather feedback from people by following these steps:

1. Go to the **Web Access** site for your team project and, in the **Activities** section of the home page, you should see a **Request feedback** link. Click on the link to start the feedback gathering process.

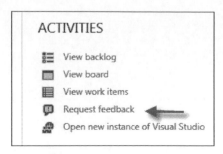

2. A dialog will appear asking you to fill in the information in three distinct sections. Section 1 is named **Select Stakeholders,** and you must enter the details of the people you want feedback from. They must be valid TFS users in order to be selected. For this recipe enter your own account here.

3. In section 2, supply the details of how users should access the application. This would typically be the details of a test site or application to install and run. Enter the address `www.packtpub.com` as the address of the web application/site.

4. In section 3, add details for the specific feedback you want from your users. Click on the **add feedback item** link to add extra items for feedback, as shown in the following screenshot:

5. Click on the **Send** button to send the e-mails to your users. Then check your e-mail. You should see a message similar to the following screenshot:

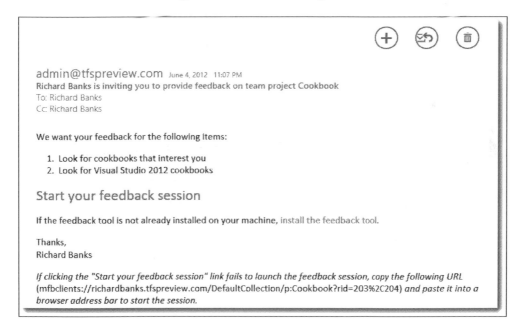

6. Because Visual Studio automatically installs the feedback client, you can just click on the **Start you feedback session** link in the e-mail. The Feedback client will then launch.

7. Click on the application link to launch the website and then click on the **Next** button in the feedback client.

8. The feedback client is now ready to accept feedback from the users, and the specific instructions you entered for the feedback session are shown.

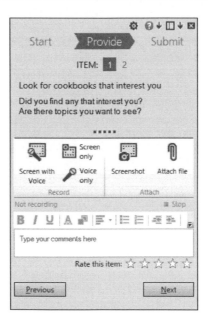

9. In the comment section, enter some text and then click on the **Screenshot** button. Select a section of the screen for your snapshot by dragging with the mouse to create a rectangle. The screenshot you take is inserted wherever the cursor is in the comments box.

10. Click on **Next** when you are ready to move to the next item. Provide more feedback if you wish and, when ready, click on the **Next** button again.

11. A summary of the feedback will be shown and you can rate each item using a five star approach. If you are happy with the feedback you have provided, click on the **Submit and Close** button to complete the feedback session.

12. Switch back to Visual Studio and, in **Team Explorer,** navigate to the **Work Items** hub and double-click on the **Feedback** query to run it.

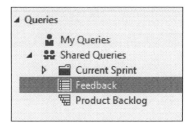

13. The query results will display all of the feedback responses received from your users. Select one of the items in the list to view the specific details of the feedback along with any images and attachments that may have been created by the feedback tool.

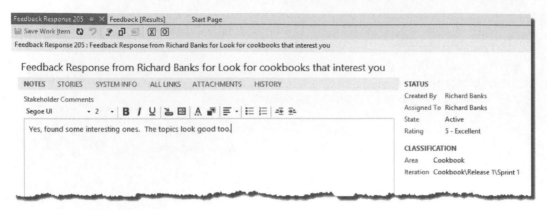

14. At this point you can create new work items based on the feedback or close the items, just as you would for any other work item.

How it works...

Under the hood, all feedback requests are stored as work items in TFS. The feedback client adds all responses as child works items linked to the feedback request.

If your users record feedback using audio or video then that data will be included as an attachment to the work item so that you can replay it when you review the responses.

There's more...

Since a picture speaks a thousand words, you can annotate your feedback screenshots by double-clicking on them once they have been added to the comments section. By default, this will open Microsoft Paint, however if you prefer different image editors such as SnagIt or Paint. NET, then you can configure this using the gear icon at the top of the feedback tool.

Visual Studio Pot Pourri

In this chapter, we will cover:

- ▸ Creating installer packages
- ▸ Submitting apps to the Windows Store
- ▸ Using the new SQL Server Data Tools
- ▸ Creating Visual Studio add-ins and extensions
- ▸ Creating your own snippets

Introduction

Just like pot pourri, this chapter is a mix of all the little things that go into Visual Studio to make it smell even nicer! The items in here don't really fit nicely with any of the previous chapters but are still very valuable and will help you in your day-to-day development activities.

Creating installer packages

With the release of Visual Studio 2010, Microsoft announced that the Visual Studio Installer project template would no longer ship with Visual Studio and, true to their word, there is no Visual Studio Installer project in Visual Studio 2012.

So, what are you meant to do if you need to create an installer package for your application?

If you are creating a Windows Store app then you don't need an installer, as the new deployment model makes installers obsolete. If you are creating a web application then Microsoft would prefer you either use XCopy deployment or the MSDeploy web deployment technology, which means installers are only required for desktop applications, and even for those there's the Click Once deployment technology to make things easier. Even then, there are a set of desktop applications that require installer packagers and if you are building one of those, Microsoft has partnered with InstallShield and included the InstallShield Limited Edition project type in Visual Studio 2012 that you can use. If you don't want to use InstallShield you can always fall back to using WiX for creating projects.

In this recipe we will use InstallShield LE to create an installer package for a simple application.

Getting ready

The recipe assumes you haven't yet installed InstallShield Limited Edition. If you have, then some of the early steps in this recipe will be different.

Simply start Visual Studio 2012, and you're ready to go.

How to do it...

Create an installer using these steps:

1. Create a new **Visual C# | WPF Application** project and name it `Simple WPF Application`.

2. Go to the project properties page by right-clicking on the project in **Solution Explorer** and selecting **Properties**. In the **Application** tab set the icon for the application to either an icon of your choice or the icon located at `C:\Program Files (x86)\ Microsoft Visual Studio 11.0\Common7\IDE\ItemTemplates\CSharp\ General\1033\Icon\Icon.ico`.

> If you are using a 32-bit operating system the path will use `Program Files` instead of `Program Files (x86)`.

3. Build the solution to make sure it compiles properly. If you have already installed InstallShield Limited Edition you can jump down to step 7.

4. Right-click on the solution and add a new project using the **Other Project Types | Setup and Deployment | Enable InstallShield Limited Edition** template.

5. A browser window will appear with instructions on how to enable InstallShield in Visual Studio 2012. Click on the link to redirect to the InstallShield website, register your details, and download the file as directed. When the download completes, save your solution, close Visual Studio 2012, and then run the InstallShield setup executable.

6. Restart Visual Studio 2012 and open the solution you created in Step 1.

7. Right-click on the solution in **Solution Explorer** and choose **Add | New Project** from the context menu. In the **Add New Project** dialog, choose **Other Project Types | InstallShield Limited Edition | InstallShield Limited Edition Project**, give it the default name, and then click on **OK**.

8. If this is the first time you have used InstallShield since it was installed you will be asked whether you wish to evaluate or register. Choose to register and activate the product using the serial number you should have received in your e-mail.

9. The InstallShield project assistant will appear in the document window.

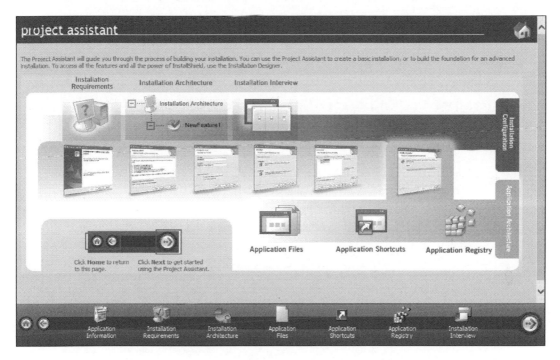

10. Click on the right arrow (the "next" button) at the bottom of the project assistant to advance to the **Application Information** page. Enter a company web address such as www.company.com.

11. Advance through the project assistant until you get to the **Application Files** page. Select the **My Product Name** node from the tree and then click on **Add Project Outputs**.

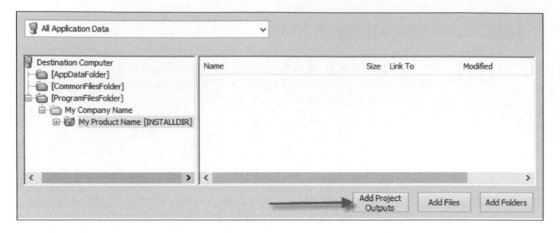

12. In the **Visual Studio Output Selector** dialog, select the **Primary output** item and click on **OK**.

13. Click on the next button to go to the **Application Shortcuts** page. Click on the **New** button to add a shortcut to your application. Choose **[ProgramFilesFolder]\My Company Name\My Product Name\Simple WPF Application.Primary output** from the dialog and click on **Open**.

14. The shortcut is named **Built** by default. That's not very useful, so click the shortcut name to edit it and rename it to Simple WPF Application.

15. Right-click on the Setup1 project in **Solution Explorer** and select **Install** from the menu. If prompted to build out of date projects, click on **Yes**.

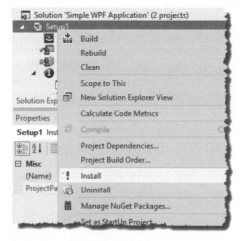

16. Step through the setup wizard to install the program. Verify that the program is installed correctly by looking for the application in your Start Menu or Start Page.

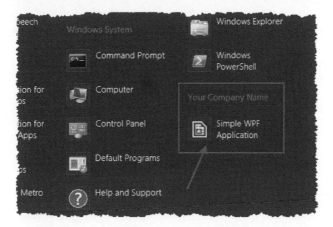

17. Remove the program from your system by right-clicking on the `Setup1` project and selecting **Uninstall**.

How it works...

InstallShield reduces the complexity in creating installers by providing a set of sensible default configuration options and an easy to use user interface. It also understands exactly how the Windows installer system works and warns when there are problems in how you have configured the installation process. For example, if you look at the warning outputs from the recipe when the package was built, you would have seen a warning about the .NET Framework and how it would be a good idea if that was included with the setup kit to ensure people who don't have .NET already installed won't have extra setup dependencies.

While you can achieve the same result using WiX, the amount of work required to get the XML written and debugged to achieve the same result would have made this a much, much longer recipe!

A license for the Limited Edition is provided free of charge with Visual Studio 2012 and will be sufficient for the basic installation purposes. If you need a heavily customized installation process then you should investigate the more advanced versions of InstallShield or competing offerings such as Nullsoft's NSIS.

Submitting apps to the Windows Store

While existing legacy desktop style applications can be distributed using current mechanisms, the only way to distribute Windows Store apps will be via the Windows Store, and they must pass a certification process for that to happen.

Enterprises and developers will be able to side-load their Windows Store apps, bypassing the store restrictions.

Getting ready

Start Visual Studio 2012 in Windows 8 and you're all set to begin.

How to do it...

Perform the following steps:

1. Start a new **Visual C# | Windows Store | Blank App (XAML)** project.

2. From the menu, select **Project | Store | Open Developer Account**.

3. A browser window will open and you can apply for a developer account using the process as outlined on the page. Windows Store accounts may require a payment of a small license fee, so have a credit card handy when you perform this step.

4. Once you have an account, switch back to Visual Studio and from the menu choose **Project | Store | Reserve app name**.

5. Again a browser window will open and you will be directed to the Windows Store to register the name for your application. Follow the process as described on that page.

6. From the Visual Studio menu, select **Project | Store | Edit App Manifest** and use the information from the app name reservation to populate the appropriate fields. Take particular note of the fields on the packaging tab.

7. Alternatively you can select the **Project | Store | Associate App with the Store** menu entry and follow the steps of the wizard to automatically populate the packaging tab with the appropriate values.

8. Write your application. No, really you should. There is no point submitting an application that does nothing.

9. Verify your application using the Windows App Certification Kit. Refer to the *Validating your Windows Store app* recipe in *Chapter 2, Getting Started with Windows Store Applications* to do this.

10. Package your application for uploading to the store by choosing **Project | Store | Create App Package**.

11. Upload the package to the store by selecting **Project | Store | Upload App Package** from the menu and following the steps presented in the ensuing upload wizard.

12. Once the upload completes you can monitor the progress of your package through the approval process using the tools provided by the store.

How it works...

The Store submenu is only available when running Visual Studio in Windows 8 and when you have opened the solution for a Windows Store app.

When you upload a package to the store there are a number of basic sanity checks to verify your package is acceptable and meets the requirements of the Windows Store. These checks include running the certification toolkit on your app and verifying the manifest information against the information you supplied when you registered the app name. Using Visual Studio's **Associate app with the store** wizard is an easy way to make sure you don't have any typographical errors in your manifest and it improves the chances of a successful first time submission.

There's more...

If you want to make money with Windows Store apps you aren't limited solely to upfront purchase revenues.

You can also distribute your app using a trial mode that encourages a try before you buy approach, provides functionality for in-app purchases, in-app advertising using any ad platform you choose, and you can even implement you own transaction system if you so desire.

For in-app purchases and trial versions of your product, Microsoft bundles supporting functionality in the `Windows.ApplicationModel.Store` namespace to make it easier for you to build applications with these features.

If you want to confirm what are the requirements for App certification refer to the Microsoft documentation on the subject at `http://msdn.microsoft.com/en-us/library/windows/apps/hh694083.aspx`.

See also

▶ The *Packaging your Windows Store app* recipe, *Chapter 2, Getting Started with Windows Store Applications*

▶ The *Validating your Windows Store app* recipe, *Chapter 2, Getting Started with Windows Store Applications*

Using the new SQL Server Data Tools

Visual Studio 2012 has removed the old Visual Studio Database Project type (also known as DataDude) and replaced it with the new SQL Server Database Project type, powered by the new SQL Server Data Tools (SSDT) and including support for SQL Server 2012 and SQL Server Azure.

There's a lot we could cover here but we'll keep it short and you can go exploring for yourself once you've cooked up this particular recipe.

For this recipe, you're just going to create the simplest of database definitions and deploy it so that you can see how the basic operations are performed.

Getting ready

You will need a SQL Server database server for this recipe, and you will need to have permissions to deploy to it. A SQL 2012 Express database is included with the Visual Studio 2012 installation and is recommended for use with this recipe.

Make a note of the connection string for your database. If you are using SQL 2012 Express then it is most likely `(localdb)\Database1` or something very similar. You can confirm this by using **SQL Server Object Explorer** in Visual Studio, as shown in the following screenshot:

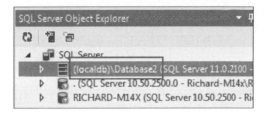

How to do it...

Create a database using the following steps:

1. Create a new **SQL Server | SQL Server Database Project** project using the default name.

2. Right-click on the project in **Solution Explorer** and from the context menu select **Add | Table**. Leave the table name as `Table1` and click on **Add**.

3. `Table1.sql` will be added and the designer will be opened in the document area. Just like the previous database projects, a declarative approach to creating databases is used.

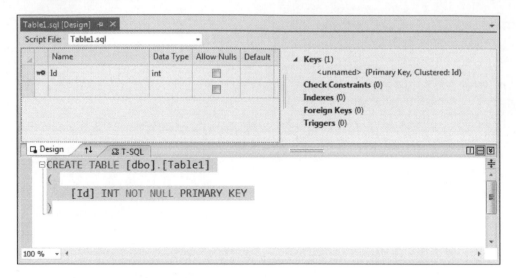

4. In the designer, add a column to the table called `Description` with a type of `nvarchar(50)` and turn off the `Allow Nulls` flag. As you do so, the T-SQL in the designer will be updated to reflect the changes you have made.

5. Build the project and look at the **Build** information in the **Output** window. You should see that both a `.dll` file and a `.dacpac` file were created as part of the build process.

6. Assume `Table1` is designed to store reference data for an application. In other words the table must be populated when the database is deployed or it will be invalid. Right-click on the project and from the context menu select **Add | Script**, then choose **Post-Deployment Script**. Leave the name as the default and click on **Add**.

7. In the script, add the following T-SQL code to populate the table with the values you want:

```
MERGE INTO Table1 AS Target
USING (VALUES
   (0, N'Zero'),
   (1, N'More than Zero')
)
AS Source (Id, Description)
ON Target.Id = Source.Id

-- update matched rows
WHEN MATCHED THEN
UPDATE SET Description = Source.Description

-- insert new rows
WHEN NOT MATCHED BY TARGET THEN
INSERT (Id, Description) VALUES (Id, Description)

-- delete rows that are in the target but not the source
WHEN NOT MATCHED BY SOURCE THEN
DELETE;
```

8. Right-click on the project in **Solution Explorer** and select **Publish**.

9. In the **Publish Database** dialog box click on **Edit** to define the connection string for the database you will deploy to, confirm the **Database name** is correct and then click **Publish**.

 If you don't have a SQL 2012 database available for use you can change the Target Platform to match your database server version in the project's property pages.

How it works...

While it should be familiar to developers who used the previous Visual Studio Database Projects (also known as DataDude), the changes under the hood for SSDT are significant. Not only does it support two new data platforms, but it also sports a new deployment model and the new DacPac format that can either be imported directly into a SQL 2012 database or applied using the SqlPackage command-line tool that comes with the database server.

The SQL Server Data Tools are intended to be a replacement for SQL Server Management Studio, so you should find that SQL Server Object Explorer provides you with much the same level of functionality as you are used to in Management Studio, albeit with a different manner of getting to that functionality.

Creating Visual Studio add-ins and extensions

When Microsoft released Visual Studio 2010 they changed the approach to extensibility by introducing the VSIX format and the number of extensions in the Visual Studio gallery is a testament to how successful this change has been.

So, what do you do if you want to make your own add-ins and extensions in Visual Studio? This recipe will walk you through that process, though the magic that happens inside the add-in or extension is up to you!

Getting ready

To create extensions you will need the Visual Studio 2012 SDK, which you can download from Microsoft.

Once the SDK is installed, start Visual Studio 2012 and you're ready to go.

How to do it...

Perform the following steps:

1. Start a new project using the **Other Project Types | Extensibility | Visual Studio Add-in** project type and the default name.

2. The **Add-in Wizard** will launch. Click on **Next** on the first page.

3. Choose the language you want to develop in. For the recipe choose **C#** and click on **Next**.

4. Click on **Next** to choose the default **Application Host** (which will be Visual Studio 2012).

5. Provide a name and description for the add-in if you are feeling creative, otherwise just click on **Next**.

6. Click on **Next** to take the defaults for the **Add-in Options**, click on **Next** again to skip the **Help About** information, and finally click on **Finish**.

7. The wizard will generate an application skeleton including all of the necessary references for building Visual Studio 2012 add-ins.

8. At this point you can go and make magic by implementing your application.

9. Pressing *F5* will start a new instance of Visual Studio in debug mode (it may take a while to start) where you can use the Add-in manager to enable your add-in and check its functionality. For now, leave the add-in as it is so you can move on to creating an extension.

10. Add a new project to your solution using the **Visual C# | Extensibility | Editor Viewport Adornment** template, leaving the name as the default. If this option isn't available check if you have installed the Visual Studio SDK correctly.

11. Open the `source.extension.vsixmanifest` file and populate the **Author** field with your name.

12. Set the new extension project as the default startup project and press *F5* to start debugging. A new instance of Visual Studio will be launched using the **experimental hive**. The experimental hive is a separate set of Visual Studio settings you can use when testing extensions that won't affect your normal development settings.

 Because a debugger is attached, starting the experimental instance of Visual Studio may take longer than you are used to.

13. When Visual Studio has finished loading it will automatically instantiate the extension making it active and available. From the Visual Studio menu, select **File | New File | File**, select **General | Text File**, and on click **Open**. You should see a purple box at the top-right of the editor surface, proving that the extension is working as expected.

14. Close the experimental instance of Visual Studio.

How it works...

There's a big difference between add-ins and extensions in Visual Studio. Add-ins are the old way of extending Visual Studio and are fairly complex to build, whereas Extensions are the preferred approach from Visual Studio 2010 onwards and are much easier to implement.

An add-in has to implement an extensibility interface and, while this means your add-in can work with Visual Studio versions prior to 2010, it is limited to functionality exposed by the DTE interfaces and as a developer you have to deal with a number of COM interfaces. An extension, on the other hand, has to implement a Managed Extensibility Framework (MEF) contract and is not as restricted in the API's it can access or in the way it is implemented.

There's more...

There is a lot more flexibility in building extensions over add-ins and this also applies to the update and distribution mechanism, however if you really need to get to the internals of Visual Studio or you need to support Visual Studio 2008 or earlier then you will need to look at the add-in approach.

The **Extension Manager** introduced with Visual Studio 2010 is the way extensions are distributed and it becomes even more central to a great Visual Studio 2012 experience as Microsoft is now distributing Visual Studio updates via the extension manager. If you look at the **Updates** section you will see categories for **Visual Studio Gallery** and **Samples Gallery**, as well as a new one for **Product Updates**. When new updates for Visual Studio are available they will appear in this area though it's still up to you as to whether you install them or not.

 When you complete the recipe, if you want to remove all trace of your add-in from Visual Studio remove the `.addin` file from `Documents\ Visual Studio 2012\Addins`.

Creating your own snippets

Visual Studio snippets are a great way to quickly write repetitive chunks of code using the same basic structure and can save you a lot of time and typing.

In Visual Studio 2012, snippets have been extended to work on more than just standard code files, so whenever you find yourself writing repetitive code and thinking "I've typed this sort of thing before!", then you are probably looking at a piece of code that could be turned into a code snippet.

For example, you may want to generate a class signature that inherits from a specific base class you use in your application, or you may have a certain attribute that needs to be placed above method calls to enable logging, or you may have specific IDs you want to use in HTML elements to ensure CSS styles can be consistently applied to your web pages.

Unfortunately Visual Studio still doesn't have an inbuilt way of authoring your own snippets so you will have to use XML. Fortunately it only takes a few minutes to create a snippet and the time you can save once it exists makes it worth doing.

This recipe will show you how to create your own snippets and make them available inside Visual Studio.

Getting ready

Simply start Visual Studio 2012 and you're ready to go.

How to do it...

Create your own snippet using the following steps:

1. From the menu, choose **File | New | File**, select **XML File**, and click on **Open**.

2. Populate the file using the following XML code:

```xml
<?xml version="1.0" encoding="utf-8"?>
<CodeSnippets
    xmlns="http://schemas.microsoft.com/VisualStudio/2005/CodeSnippet">
  <CodeSnippet Format="1.0.0">
    <Header>
      <Title>Wrap text in a span</Title>
      <Shortcut>spanned</Shortcut>
      <SnippetTypes>
        <SnippetType>Expansion</SnippetType>
        <SnippetType>SurroundsWith</SnippetType>
      </SnippetTypes>
    </Header>
    <Snippet>
      <Declarations>
        <Literal>
          <ID>id</ID>
          <Default>elementId</Default>
        </Literal>
      </Declarations>
      <Code Language="HTML">
        <![CDATA[
        <span id="$id$">$selected$</span> $end$ is now in a span!
        ]]>
      </Code>
    </Snippet>
  </CodeSnippet>
</CodeSnippets>
```

3. Save the file as `spanned text.snippet` in your `Documents` folder.

4. From the menu, select **Tools | Code Snippets Manager**.

5. Click on the **Import** button. Select the file you saved in step 3 and click on **OK**.

6. Leave the location as **My HTML Snippets,** as suggested, and click on **Finish**. The snippet file will be automatically copied to the appropriate location in `Documents\ Visual Studio 2012\Code Snippets`.

7. In the **Snippet Manager,** change the **Language** to **HTML** and expand the **My HTML Snippets** location to confirm your snippet has been loaded.

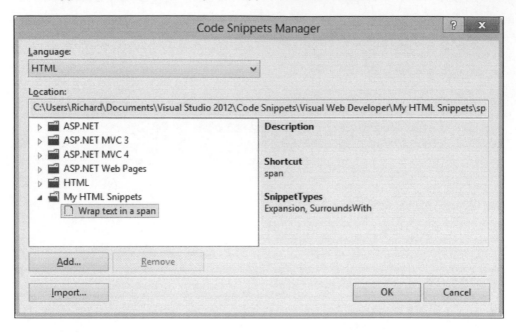

8. From the menu, select **File | New | File**, select **General | HTML Page**, and click on **Open**.

9. In the contents of the body tag, enter `<p>this is some text</p>`.

10. Select the words `is some`. Right-click on the selection, choose **Surround With**, then **My HTML Snippets | Wrap text in a span**, and hit *Enter*.

11. The snippet will be expanded and the contents of the `id` attribute for the `span` will be selected. Enter the text `myId` to replace the highlighted `elementId` placeholder and hit *Enter*.

12. The cursor will move to the end of the closing `span` tag.

How it works...

The `Declarations` section of the snippet defined `id` as a `Literal` variable. By declaring the snippet as an `Expansion` snippet, Visual Studio automatically scanned the code body of the snippet for an identifier placeholder of `$id$` so that it could populate it with the default value and prompt you for your own value.

By declaring the snippet as a `SurroundsWith` snippet, the selected text is passed to the `$selected$` placeholder in the body, and when the snippet completes the `$end$` placeholder indicates where the cursor should be positioned.

There's more...

There is a Snippet Designer project on Codeplex (`http://snippetdesigner.codeplex.com/`) that offers a GUI tool to make creating snippets much easier. It also enables you to select a section of code and export that as a snippet so that you have an easy starting point for making your own custom snippets.

Remember that snippets are more than just a simple text entry/replacement mechanism and it's worth spending a little time looking through the full schema reference for snippets on MSDN at `http://msdn.microsoft.com/en-us/library/ms171418(VS.110).aspx` to get a better idea of what they can do for you.

Index

Symbols

3D model
  creating 191
  creating, steps for 192-194
  working 194
3D Model support 29
[Bindable] attribute 175
-moz- attribute 74
.NET applications
  unit testing 111-115
.NET projects
  and Metro profile 39
-webkit- attribute 74

A

Aaron Powell
  URL 75
AboutUs method 223
ActionBlock object 166, 167
actors 166
add feedback item link 227
add-ins, Visual Studio
  creating 242, 243
Add Overall Comment link 224
append() method 76
App Manifest 55
ASP.NET MVC 2 projects 10
ASP.NET process
  debugging 131, 132
ASP.NET Web Stack
  URL 107
Associate app with the store wizard 238
AsyncController class 165

asynchronous code
  about 125
  creating 150
  creating, steps for 150-155
  working 155
asynchronous tests 116
asynchronous web applications
  about 161, 162
  creating, steps for 162-164
asynchronous Windows Runtime
  about 156
  steps 157-161
async keyword 153, 154, 164
async method 160
Attach to Process dialog 131, 132
Available Declarations drop down 54
await keyword 154

B

Basic Page item template 43
Blank App template 35
Blank layout 215
bundling 79-83

C

C++
  about 171
  data binding 175
  XAML, using 172-175
Calculator class 113
Calculator() constructor 113
capabilities
  about 52
  Home or Work Networking capability 58

Internet (Client) capability 57
Internet (Client & Server) capability 58
C++ applications
unit testing 175-179
C++ code
analyzing 180
analyzing, steps for 180-182
working 182
class libraries
portable class libraries 117
sharing, across runtimes 117-119
Class Library project 38
C++ Metro apps 39
code
in production, debugging 133-138
making asynchronous 150
old search dialog 25
regular expressions, using 25
searching 23
searching, steps for 24
code reviews
performing 219
performing, steps for 220-230
CoffeeBundler package 108
Color Picker button 71
color property 73
COM Interop 39
commands, Visual Studio
finding 16-19
Common category 216
Complete() method 169
concurrency visualizer
about 144
improvements 144-147
working 148
Console.ReadKey() statement 129
contents variable 153
Continuous Testing 112
contract picker 56
contracts
about 52
contract picker 56
file open picker 56
File Type Associations contarct 57
search contarct 56
share target contarct 57

CSS bundling 79-83
CSS editor
improvements 70-74
CubeRenderer$$Render() method 186
C# Workflows 102

D

DataDude. *See* **Studio Database Project type**
declaration 53
Declarations section 246
DGSL (Directed Graph Shader Language)
about 29, 186
used, for creating shader 186-190
Direct2D App (XAML) template 38
Direct3D App template 38
DirectX acceleration 29
DirectX application 172
DirectX, Visual Studio 2012
working with 182-185
DLL (Metro style apps) template 38
DownloadStringTaskAsync() method 155
duplicate code
detecting 119-121
working 122

E

editor windows
managing 11-14
Effect property 193
existing solution
upgrading 8-10
Extension Manager 244
extensions, Visual Studio
creating 242, 243

F

feedback
getting, from users 225-229
Filename property 193
File Open Picker Contract item template 43
file picker contract 56
File Type Associations contract 57
Final Color node 190
Find button 132

Find in Files option 102
Find tool 23
Fixed Layout App template 37
for loop 130

G

go() function 77
go() method 78
Graphics Pipeline Stages window 199
graphic tools
  3D Model support 29
  MIP mapping 29
  pixel shaders 29
  using 25-27
Grid App tcmplate 35-37
Group Detail Page item template 43
Grouped Items Page item template 43

H

hierarchical indentation feature 72
HLSL shaders 29
Home or Work Networking capability 58
HTML5 web pages
  about 66
  creating, steps for 66-69
  working 69
HttpClient class 156, 160

I

IIS Express
  about 65
  URL 66
INotifyPropertyChanged interface 175
Install button 108
installer packages
  creating 231
  creating, steps for 232-235
  working 235
InstallShield 235
IntelliTrace 133
Internet (Client) capability 57
Internet (Client & Server) capability 58
Item Detail Page item template 43
ItemListView_SelectionChanged() method 50
Items Page item template 43

J

JavaScript editor
  improvements 75-78
  regions 79
  working 78
jumpy rotation 186

L

library access 58
LinkTo() method 169
LoadFeeds button 159
LoadFeeds.Click event handler 160
local workspaces
  using, for source control 207-213

M

Main() method 151, 185
MainPage class 174
Managed Extensibility Framework. *See* MEF
margin-top attribute 87
MEF 166
Metro app
  validating 63, 64
Metro item templates
  adding, to app 40-42
  Basic Page item template 43
  File Open Picker Contract item template 43
  Group Detail Page item template 43
  Grouped Items Page item template 43
  Item Detail Page item template 43
  Items Page item template 43
  Search Contract item template 43
  Share Target Contract item template 43
  Split Page item template 43
  technology choices 44
Metro profile
  and .NET projects 39
Metro project types
  about 35
  Blank App template 35
  Class Library project 38
  Direct2D App (XAML) template 38
  Direct3D App template 38
  DLL (Metro style apps) template 38
  Fixed Layout App template 37

Grid App template 35-37
Navigation App template 37
Split App template 37
Static Library (Metro style apps) template 38
technology choices 38
Unit Test Library project 38
Windows Runtime Component 38
Metro style apps
about 7, 31, 32
notifications 62
package, signing 62
packaging 58
packaging, steps for 59-61
working 62
Microsoft Native Minimum Rules rule set 182
Microsoft Native Recommended Rules rule set 182
Microsoft website
URL 126
minification 79-83
MIP mapping 29
m_isRotating flag 184
MSDN
snippets, URL 247
MSTest 111, 112
multithreaded code 125
MyColor class 175

N

navigating 19-23
Navigation App template 37
NuGet
packages, managing with 107-109
working 110, 111

O

office projects 7
old search dialog 25
OnLaunched method 41
opacity code snippet 73

P

packages
managing, with NuGet 107-109

PageAsyncTask object 163
Page_Init() method 163
page inspector
used, for verifying pages 84-87
Page_Load() method 20
Page_OrientationChanged() method 50
Page_PreRender() method 164
pages
partial pages and user control 88
verifying, page inspector used 84-87
panning 102
parallel code
debugging 139
debugging, steps for 140-143
working 143
Parallel.For loop 165
Parallel LINQ. *See* **PLINQ**
Parse() method 153
partial pages
and user control 88
Pending Changes hub 212
pipeline 166
Pixel History icon 196
pixel shaders 29
PLINQ 139
PointerEventArgs class 185
Portable Class Library project 7, 117
Preview Selected Items button 14, 15
private variable 183
ProcessFeedsAsync method 155
ProcessFeedsAsync() method 154
production code
debugging 133-138
project
and operating system 7
new project, creating 5-7
new project, types 7
office projects 7
Portable Class Library project 7
retired project templates 7
Promote as Rename option 212
PublishedDate() method 151, 159

Q

Qualifier drop down 132
Quick Access Toolbar 94

Quick Find option 102
Quick Launch control 19

R

ReadFeed() helper method 159
ReadFeed() method 151, 153, 163
ReadKey() method 129, 154, 155
RegisterBundles() method 81
remote machines
    debugging on 126-131
retired project templates 7
ribbon
    adding, to WPF 92-96
RibbonTab button 96
RotatingCube$$Run() method 184
round tripping 8
runtimes
    class libraries, sharing 117-119

S

Scripts.Render() statement 81
search contract 56
Search Contract item template 43
searching 19-23
setTimeout method 77
shader
    about 191
    creating, DGSL used 186-190
Shader property 193
Share Target Contract item template 43, 57
SharpDX
    URL 186
Silverlight 3 11
single click preview
    in Solution Explorer 14
SkyDrive app 56
SkyDrive storage space 32
SmallImageSource attribute 96
smart pointer 175
Snippet Designer project
    URL 247
snippets, Visual Studio
    creating 244-246
Solution Explorer
    single click preview 14

source control
    local workspaces, using 207-213
Split App template 34, 37
Split Page item template 43
SQL Server Data Tools
    database creating, steps for 239, 240
    using 239
    working 241
Start Debugging menu option 45
Start you feedback session link 228
state machine
    creating, in Visual Studio 2012 97-102
Static Library (Metro style apps) template 38
storyboarding
    about 214
    creating, steps for 215-217
    working 217
Storyboard Shapes tool window 215
Studio Database Project type 239
Style property editor 71

T

tab
    customizing 15
tablets
    debugging on 126-131
Task Parallel Library. *See* TPL
Task<string> object 153
Task.WhenAll method 154, 160
Team Explorer tool 203
Team Foundation Server 2012. *See* TFS
TestSettings files 115
textwidth() method 76
TFS
    about 201
    code reviews, performing 219-225
    feedback, getting from users 225-230
    local workspaces, using for source control
        207-212
    used, for managing work 202-205
Thread.Sleep method 144
Title Slide layout 215
TPL 139
    about 165
TPL Dataflow Library
    about 165

creating 166-168
working 169
TransformBlock object 166, 167
trim() method 79

U

unit testing
.NET applications 111-115
C++ applications 175-179
running, in debug mode 180
Unit Test Library project 38
user control
and partial pages 88
users
feedback, getting from 225-230

V

variable values 139
Visual Studio
database projects 10
Visual Studio 2012
about 5
DirectX, working with 182-185
new project, creating 5-7
state machine, creating 97-102
Visual Studio add-ins
creating 242, 243
Visual Studio commands
finding 16-19
Visual Studio extensions
creating 242, 243
Visual Studio Graphics Debugger
using 194-197
working 198
Visual Studio snippets
creating 244-246

W

WCF service, task-based
creating 103
creating, steps for 103-106
working 106
web applications
and asynchrony 161, 162

WebClient class 156
window
customizing 15
Windows 8 Metro app
about 33
creating, steps for 34
Metro item template, adding 40-42
submitting, to Windows store 236, 237
Windows 8 simulator
about 44, 45
location settings 52
remote debugging 51
resizing 51
resolution 51
screenshots, taking 52
using, steps for 45-50
working 50
Windows Presentation Foundation. *See* **WPF**
Windows RT 32
Windows Runtime
about 7
and asynchrony 156, 157
development technology, selecting 33
Windows Runtime Component 38
Windows store
Windows 8 Metro app, submitting to 236, 237
WinRT. *See* **Windows Runtime**
work
managing 202
managing, TFS used 202-206
managing, Visual Studio 2012 used 202-206
WorkflowIdentity class 103
workflows
versioning 103
Work Item form 204
Work Item Search field 206
WPF
about 92
ribbon, adding 92-96

X

XAML
using, with C++ 172-175
xamltypeinfo.g.cpp 175

[PACKT] Thank you for buying
PUBLISHING

Visual Studio 2012 Cookbook

About Packt Publishing

Packt, pronounced 'packed', published its first book "*Mastering phpMyAdmin for Effective MySQL Management*" in April 2004 and subsequently continued to specialize in publishing highly focused books on specific technologies and solutions.

Our books and publications share the experiences of your fellow IT professionals in adapting and customizing today's systems, applications, and frameworks. Our solution based books give you the knowledge and power to customize the software and technologies you're using to get the job done. Packt books are more specific and less general than the IT books you have seen in the past. Our unique business model allows us to bring you more focused information, giving you more of what you need to know, and less of what you don't.

Packt is a modern, yet unique publishing company, which focuses on producing quality, cutting-edge books for communities of developers, administrators, and newbies alike. For more information, please visit our website: www.packtpub.com.

Writing for Packt

We welcome all inquiries from people who are interested in authoring. Book proposals should be sent to author@packtpub.com. If your book idea is still at an early stage and you would like to discuss it first before writing a formal book proposal, contact us; one of our commissioning editors will get in touch with you.

We're not just looking for published authors; if you have strong technical skills but no writing experience, our experienced editors can help you develop a writing career, or simply get some additional reward for your expertise.

Software Testing using Visual Studio 2010

ISBN: 978-1-849681-40-7   Paperback: 400 pages

A step-by-step guide to understand the features and concepts of testing applications using Visual Studio.

1. Master all the new tools and techniques in Visual Studio 2010 and the Team Foundation Server for testing applications

2. Customize reports with Team foundation server

3. Get to grips with the new Test Manager tool for maintaining Test cases

4. Take full advantage of new Visual Studio features for testing an application's User Interface

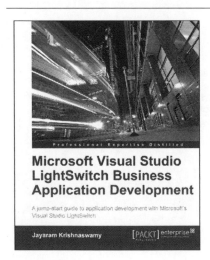

Microsoft Visual Studio LightSwitch Business Application Development

ISBN: 978-1-849682-86-2   Paperback: 384 pages

A jump-start guide to application development with Microsoft's Visual Studio LightSwitch

1. A hands-on guide, packed with screenshots and step-by-step instructions and relevant background information—making it easy to build your own application with this book and ebook

2. Easily connect to various data sources with practical examples and easy-to-follow instructions

3. Create entities and screens both from scratch and using built-in templates

Please check **www.PacktPub.com** for information on our titles

Microsoft SharePoint 2010 Development with Visual Studio 2010: Expert Cookbook

ISBN: 978-1-849684-58-3   Paperback: 296 pages

Develop, debug, and deploy business solutions for SharePoint applications using Visual Studio 2010

1. Create applications using the latest client object model and create custom web services for your SharePoint environment with this book and ebook.

2. Full of illustrations, diagrams and key points for debugging and deploying your solutions securely to the SharePoint environment.

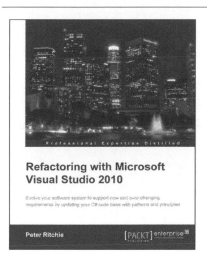

Refactoring with Microsoft Visual Studio 2010

ISBN: 978-1-849680-10-3   Paperback: 372 pages

Evolve your software system to support new and ever-changing requirements by updating your C# code base with patterns and principles

1. Make your code base maintainable with refactoring

2. Support new features more easily by making your system adaptable

3. Enhance your system with an improved object-oriented design and increased encapsulation and componentization

Please check **www.PacktPub.com** for information on our titles

Printed in Great Britain
by Amazon.co.uk, Ltd.,
Marston Gate.